ECONOMIC ISSUES, PROBLEMS AND PERSPECTIVES

PERILS OF PURCHASING PRECIOUS METALS AND COINS

Economic Issues, Problems and Perspectives

Additional books in this series can be found on Nova's website under the Series tab.

Additional e-books in this series can be found on Nova's website under the e-book tab.

ECONOMIC ISSUES, PROBLEMS AND PERSPECTIVES

PERILS OF PURCHASING PRECIOUS METALS AND COINS

GIOVANNI KINSEY
EDITOR

NOVINKA

New York

For permission to use material from this book please contact us:
Telephone 631-231-7269; Fax 631-231-8175
Web Site: http://www.novapublishers.com

Library of Congress Cataloging-in-Publication Data

ISBN: 978-1-62081-154-2

Published by Nova Science Publishers, Inc. † New York

CONTENTS

PREFACE

Precious metals are a class of metals deemed rare or highly valued, such as gold, silver, palladium, and platinum. Such metals can be bought and sold in the form of bullion bars, ingots, or coins. Due to the size and weight of the goods, investment firms typically transfer the title of the metal instead of the metal itself, which often remains in storage under the care of the firm or its affiliates. Like all commodities, the price of precious metals fluctuates. Still, the metals are perceived to be the safest form of investment, as they can be less volatile than the stock market. This book discusses the perils of the precious metals market. This also includes investing in bullion and bullion coins and collectible coins.

Chapter 1 – Precious metals are a class of metals deemed rare or highly valued, such as gold, silver, palladium, and platinum. Since the advent of exchange-traded funds for these metals in the early 2000s, demand for precious metals jumped significantly. Then, when the 2008 financial crisis hit, the allure of precious metals as a relatively safe investment grew even more.

As more and more Americans sought the safety of precious metals, thieves, con-men, and swindlers entered the retail market looking for an easy buck. They lured seniors and other populations with tall tales of quick riches, endless profitability, and privileged information. Consumers were told that precious metals were immune from market volatility, even though commodity prices are subject to the general fits and starts of supply and demand. In 2013 alone, the price of gold fell nearly 30 percent.

Some of the telemarketing firms that sold retail precious metals worked with seedy suppliers to defraud consumers by either taking customer money without any intention to deliver the metals, or applying the transaction on paper only—through derivative contracts, such as gold futures. Although customers were led to believe they owned the metals outright, many of them in fact only owned a stake in a derivatives contract held by the company, and they suffered the first loss if the metal declined in value.

Many of these firms convinced would-be consumers that an impending jump in the price of a metal was right around the corner, getting them to act fast on supposed privileged information, which in some cases was found to be contrived out of thin air. Customers were also pressed to store the metals they purchased in an account not under their control, rather than take physical delivery of the metal. The firm could then charge storage fees on top of commission and account fees, and any price markup charged by the supplier. Remarkably, in some cases, Committee staff found storage fees were applied even though no metal was actually stored on behalf of the customer.

Disreputable retail precious metal companies use various tactics to extract as much money from their customers as possible, including pressuring them to use in-house credit to buy more of the metals. Through this financial arrangement, the company can charge interest expenses on the total metal value even though the customer never takes physical possession of it. In some of these cases, customers are not told—either before or after the sale—about the risks involved in such financial arrangements, and the possibility they may end up with negative equity if the price of the metal declines and they are subject to a margin call that puts them on the hook for the remaining balance of the loan. In fact, these financed transactions make it nearly impossible for customers to get a return on their investment.

Recently the Federal Trade Commission (FTC) and the Commodity Futures Trading Commission (CFTC) have stepped up efforts to combat the worst practices in the industry. Generally, the FTC has gone after nefarious retail precious metal dealers that use high-pressure sales tactics to deceive consumers into believing they'll earn substantial profits in a short period of time. Some of them may also hide or understate the risk involved with the purchase, or fail to disclose all the fees and commissions charged.

Meanwhile, the Dodd-Frank Wall Street Reform and Consumer Protection Act (Public Law 111- 203) gave the CFTC the ability to regulate retail commodity transactions, including the sale of precious metals. In recent years, the CFTC has exercised its authority by going after precious metal companies that take customer funds without physically delivering the metals to the customer, or to a storage account under his or her control.

Even though the federal government has stepped up enforcement actions, many unscrupulous precious metal dealers are still able to cheat customers due to a lack of transparency within the industry and relatively little monitoring of their business practices. However, local officials in Florida, Minnesota, Texas, North Carolina, and California have made progress at combating the worst practices in the industry.

During a year-long investigation into the industry by Committee staff, several precious metal firms were contacted to learn more about their practices. Although some of the firms were cooperative, a number of them employed various tactics to shield their activities from public scrutiny. Committee staff found the retail precious metals world to be incredibly limited, with a handful of salespeople and managers going from one firm to the next. In at least one case, employees who worked at one firm that was shut down by a federal regulator moved to another company to sell precious metals to customers unaware of their tainted history.

While many firms claim to not deal with seniors in any notable capacity, direct observation of their sales calls suggest they look for customers with attributes that tend to apply to seniors. During a sales call, several questions are asked to gauge the profit potential of the customer, including the age of the customer and the amount of money he or she has in a retirement account. According to state prosecutors, many firms pressure customers to use their retirement savings to buy the metals. Retirement savings are sought after because federal law allows the funds to be used on a pre-tax basis for the purchase of the metals.

Even though the law imposes strict standards for the quality of metals eligible for purchase through a retirement account, there are no restrictions on the type of financial arrangement used to purchase the metal. In other words, pre-tax retirement funds can be used to purchase precious metals financed in part with in-house credit, which has been found to be highly risky.

Committee staff conservatively estimates that more than 10,000 Americans have been victimized through these schemes, with losses around $300 million. Unfortunately, while federal and state regulators continue to be aggressive against the worst actors in the industry, many other bad actors are able to continue their shady dealings with impunity. The purpose of this staff investigation is to shed light on these schemes and help protect consumers from the perils of the precious metals market.

Chapter 2 – This is the Statement of Bill Nelson, Chairman, Senate Special Committee on Aging.

Chapter 3 – This is the Statement of Susan M. Collins, Senator, Senate Special Committee on Aging.

Chapter 4 – This is the Statement of Rosemary Hollinger, Deputy Director of the Division of Enforcement, Commodity Futures Trading Commission.

Chapter 5 – This is the Statement of Dama Brown, Director, Southwest Region, Federal Trade Commission. Hearing on "Exploring the Perils of the Precious Metals Market."

Chapter 6 – This is the Testimony of Karl Spicer, Former Precious Metals Telemarketer.

Chapter 7 – This is the Testimony of Joe Melomo, Former IBM Physicist. Hearing on "Exploring the Perils of the Precious Metals Market."

Chapter 8 – Report of the Federal Trade Commission on Investing in Bullion and Bullion Coins.

Chapter 9 – Report of the Federal Trade Commission on Investing in Collectible Coins.

In: Perils of Purchasing Precious Metals … ISBN: 978-1-62081-154-2
Editor: Giovanni Kinsey

Chapter 1

EXPLORING THE PERILS OF THE PRECIOUS METALS MARKET*

U.S. Senate Special Committee on Aging

SUMMARY

Precious metals are a class of metals deemed rare or highly valued, such as gold, silver, palladium, and platinum. Since the advent of exchange-traded funds for these metals in the early 2000s, demand for precious metals jumped significantly. Then, when the 2008 financial crisis hit, the allure of precious metals as a relatively safe investment grew even more.

As more and more Americans sought the safety of precious metals, thieves, con-men, and swindlers entered the retail market looking for an easy buck. They lured seniors and other populations with tall tales of quick riches, endless profitability, and privileged information. Consumers were told that precious metals were immune from market volatility, even though commodity prices are subject to the general fits and starts of supply and demand. In 2013 alone, the price of gold fell nearly 30 percent.

Some of the telemarketing firms that sold retail precious metals worked with seedy suppliers to defraud consumers by either taking customer money without any intention to deliver the metals, or applying the transaction on paper only—through derivative contracts, such as gold

* This is an edited, reformatted and augmented version of a Committee Staff Investigation report issued April 2014.

futures. Although customers were led to believe they owned the metals outright, many of them in fact only owned a stake in a derivatives contract held by the company, and they suffered the first loss if the metal declined in value.

Many of these firms convinced would-be consumers that an impending jump in the price of a metal was right around the corner, getting them to act fast on supposed privileged information, which in some cases was found to be contrived out of thin air. Customers were also pressed to store the metals they purchased in an account not under their control, rather than take physical delivery of the metal. The firm could then charge storage fees on top of commission and account fees, and any price markup charged by the supplier. Remarkably, in some cases, Committee staff found storage fees were applied even though no metal was actually stored on behalf of the customer.

Disreputable retail precious metal companies use various tactics to extract as much money from their customers as possible, including pressuring them to use in-house credit to buy more of the metals. Through this financial arrangement, the company can charge interest expenses on the total metal value even though the customer never takes physical possession of it. In some of these cases, customers are not told—either before or after the sale—about the risks involved in such financial arrangements, and the possibility they may end up with negative equity if the price of the metal declines and they are subject to a margin call that puts them on the hook for the remaining balance of the loan. In fact, these financed transactions make it nearly impossible for customers to get a return on their investment.

Recently the Federal Trade Commission (FTC) and the Commodity Futures Trading Commission (CFTC) have stepped up efforts to combat the worst practices in the industry. Generally, the FTC has gone after nefarious retail precious metal dealers that use high-pressure sales tactics to deceive consumers into believing they'll earn substantial profits in a short period of time. Some of them may also hide or understate the risk involved with the purchase, or fail to disclose all the fees and commissions charged.

Meanwhile, the Dodd-Frank Wall Street Reform and Consumer Protection Act (Public Law 111- 203) gave the CFTC the ability to regulate retail commodity transactions, including the sale of precious metals. In recent years, the CFTC has exercised its authority by going after precious metal companies that take customer funds without physically delivering the metals to the customer, or to a storage account under his or her control.

Even though the federal government has stepped up enforcement actions, many unscrupulous precious metal dealers are still able to cheat customers due to a lack of transparency within the industry and relatively little monitoring of their business practices. However, local officials in

Florida, Minnesota, Texas, North Carolina, and California have made progress at combating the worst practices in the industry.

During a year-long investigation into the industry by Committee staff, several precious metal firms were contacted to learn more about their practices. Although some of the firms were cooperative, a number of them employed various tactics to shield their activities from public scrutiny. Committee staff found the retail precious metals world to be incredibly limited, with a handful of salespeople and managers going from one firm to the next. In at least one case, employees who worked at one firm that was shut down by a federal regulator moved to another company to sell precious metals to customers unaware of their tainted history.

While many firms claim to not deal with seniors in any notable capacity, direct observation of their sales calls suggest they look for customers with attributes that tend to apply to seniors. During a sales call, several questions are asked to gauge the profit potential of the customer, including the age of the customer and the amount of money he or she has in a retirement account. According to state prosecutors, many firms pressure customers to use their retirement savings to buy the metals. Retirement savings are sought after because federal law allows the funds to be used on a pre-tax basis for the purchase of the metals.

Even though the law imposes strict standards for the quality of metals eligible for purchase through a retirement account, there are no restrictions on the type of financial arrangement used to purchase the metal. In other words, pre-tax retirement funds can be used to purchase precious metals financed in part with in-house credit, which has been found to be highly risky.

Committee staff conservatively estimates that more than 10,000 Americans have been victimized through these schemes, with losses around $300 million. Unfortunately, while federal and state regulators continue to be aggressive against the worst actors in the industry, many other bad actors are able to continue their shady dealings with impunity. The purpose of this staff investigation is to shed light on these schemes and help protect consumers from the perils of the precious metals market.

WHAT ARE PRECIOUS METALS?

Precious metals are a class of metals deemed rare or highly valued, such as gold, silver, palladium, and platinum.[1] Such metals can be bought and sold in the form of bullion bars, ingots, or coins.[2] Due to the size and weight of the goods, investment firms typically transfer the title of the metal instead of the metal itself, which often remains in storage under the care of the firm or its affiliates.[3]

Like all commodities, the price of precious metals fluctuates.[4] Still, the metals are perceived to be the safest form of investment, as they can be less volatile than the stock market.[5] An April 2011 Gallup poll found that 34 percent of Americans thought gold in particular was the best long-term investment, more than any other investment category, including real estate and mutual funds.[6] Precious metal sellers often use this perception to their advantage when soliciting customers. However, the public's comfort with gold may be waning, as a 2013 Gallup poll found the percent of Americans that viewed gold as the safest investment slipped from 34 to 24 percent.[7]

Unlike stocks and bonds, the value of precious metals is not based on the revenue stream or the earnings potential of an underlying asset. It is based purely on the supply and demand of the metal, whether the demand is driven by industrial uses or investment appeal. Over the last decade, the price spikes of gold and other precious metals largely coincided with the advent of commodity exchange-traded funds (ETFs), which allow small investors to jump in and out of the market quickly and cheaply.[8]

Many analysts believe it is easier to place a value on stocks and bonds—because they can be linked to dividends and interest—than it is to value gold, because its value is based on an investor's perception of its worth.[9] Although precious metals can be safe investments during periods of financial distress, their value becomes less attractive during periods of economic stability.[10]

The following graphs compare market volatility for precious metals and the stock market, as represented by the Standard & Poor's 500 (S&P 500) Index. As these graphs show, both precious metals and stocks can experience periods of volatility, and neither are immune from wild swings in the market.

Although many legitimate market analysts believe precious metals are a good way to diversify an investment portfolio,[11] they warn that investments in precious metals only make sense if an investor has money he or she does not need right away.[12] Unfortunately, unscrupulous precious metal dealers who are the subject of this investigation have often manipulated those with very limited resources, especially senior citizens, into moving all of their assets into unfavorable precious metal transactions, riddled with high fees, commissions, and other hidden costs.[13]

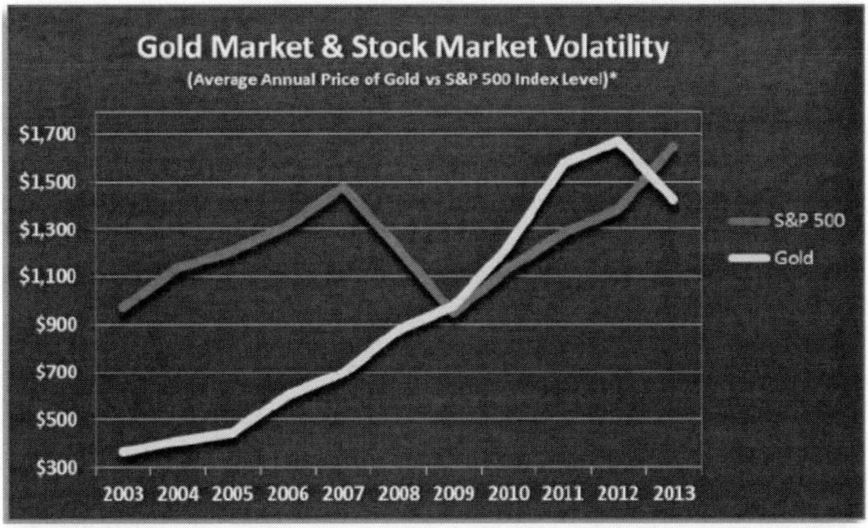

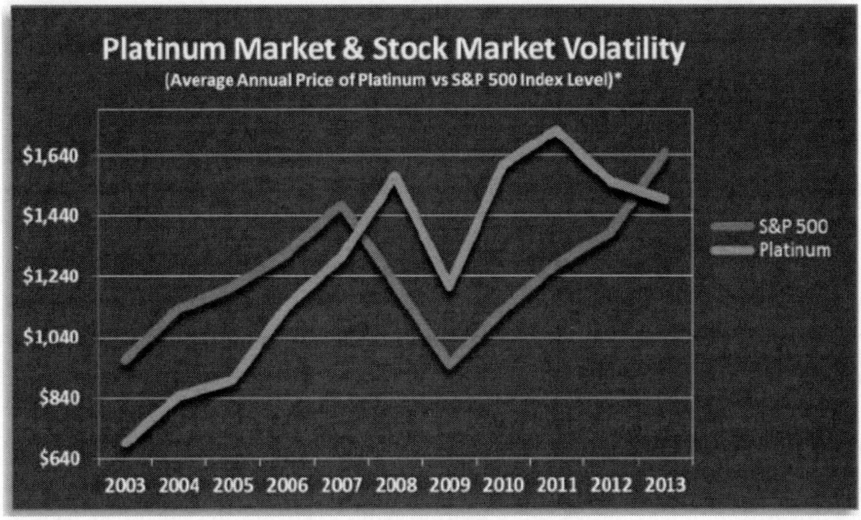

*Source: Kitco Metals Inc. (kitco.com) and Yahoo Finance.

Both Precious Metals and Stocks Experience Volatility.

THE PILLARS OF FRAUD & DECEPTION

Retail precious metal scams often involve several firms acting in unison to extract as much money from a customer as possible.[14] One firm acts as a telemarketer, known as the introducing firm, often soliciting retail investors through high-pressure sales tactics.[15] Once the customer decides to invest in the precious metal, his or her information is passed on to a separate, but affiliated entity, known as a wholesale dealer.[16] Wholesale dealers are supposed to buy the metal from a distributor and ship it directly to the customer, or store the metal on the customer's behalf.[17] In exchange, the introducing firm shares a percentage of its fees with the wholesale dealer.[18] The wholesale dealer also typically charges a spread of 3 to 5 percent of the current market price of the metal.[19]

The introducing firm typically charges a commission for the transaction, which can amount to 15 percent of the total metal value, in addition to any fees associated with opening an account, storing the metal, or delivery of the metal.[20] In some cases, customers are charged storage fees even though no metal is stored on their behalf.[21] In such cases, customers are led to believe they own the metal, but in reality the wholesale dealer may only cover the purchase on paper through offsetting derivatives[22]—such as futures, forwards, and rolling spot contracts.[23] In some cases customer purchases are "covered" by giving them a direct stake in the derivatives, through which the customer receives the first loss if the derivative declines in value.[24]

Many of the retail precious metal companies involved in these scams also offer in-house credit to help customers buy metals through "leveraged" or "financed" transactions.[25] In such cases, the customer usually pays 20 to 25 percent of the full metal cost, with the remainder financed through in-house credit.[26] The customer is responsible for paying back the full amount of the loan, plus interest.[27]

Since the purchased metals act as collateral for the loan, leveraged transactions add more risk to the investment, even though many customers believe they wholly own the metals and can wait out any downturn in the market.[28] However, in a leveraged transaction if the value of the metal depreciates below a minimum threshold – typically 10 percent[29] – the investment account is subject to a margin call, requiring the customer to buy more of the metal to maintain the equity in the account.[30] If the customer cannot cover the margin call, the account is usually liquidated— without customer permission—to cover the remaining balance of the loan.[31]

While leveraged transactions increase the profitability of precious metal firms, it is nearly impossible for consumers to make a profit from such transactions.[32] In fact, with all the hidden charges attached, they can easily end up with a loss greater than their initial investment.

Here's an example, as illustrated in the following graphic: A customer buys $10,000 worth of gold through a leveraged transaction. He covers 20 percent of the cost by putting $2,000 down. The firm finances the remaining $8,000, charging the customer 9.5% interest, or $760 annually.

The firm also charges him a 15% commission, totaling $1,500 in addition to $200 in other fees. Interest payments aside, the customer is already out $3,700 from the start. If the value of the gold drops below the value of the loan plus interest ($8,760), the metal is automatically liquidated and the customer loses that $3,700 with no gold to show for it.[33]

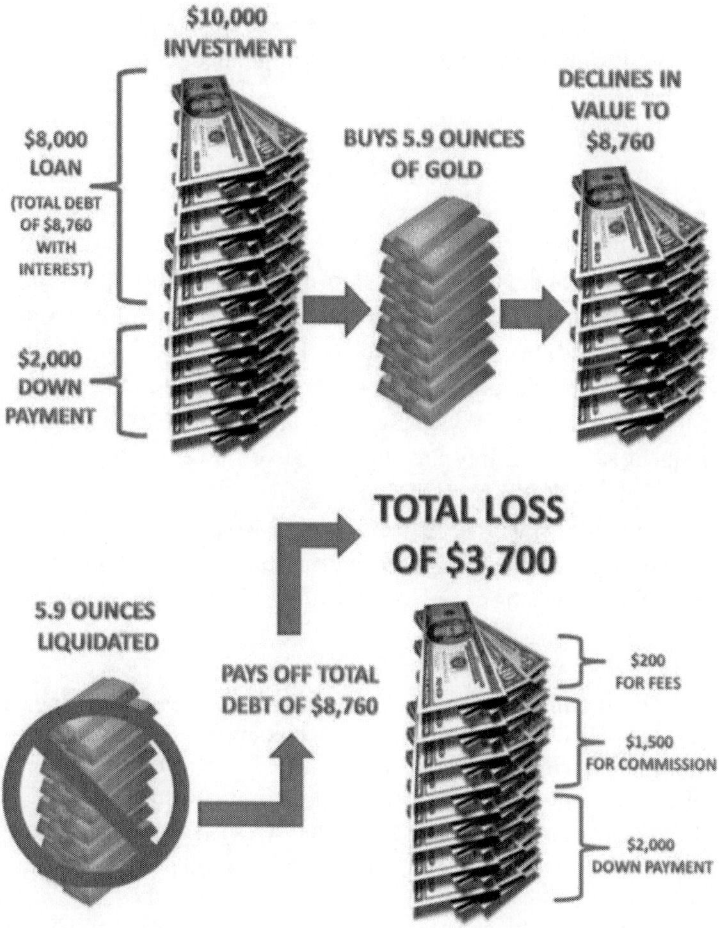

How Customers Lose Out on Leveraged Transactions.

In this scenario, the customer would only make money if the value of the gold increased to cover storage and service fees, commission costs, and the cost of the loan plus interest; without first experiencing any significant decline in price. Unfortunately, the market for precious metals is not immune to volatility, as changing expectations can lead to significant swings in the market. In 2013 alone, the price of gold fell nearly 30 percent.[34]

While many investment firms try to steer their customers toward financial safety, several precious metal companies have been found to lead nearly all of their customers to financial ruin through a gamut of fees, debt expenses, and commission charges. [35] For example, since it commenced operations, wholesale dealer Hunter Wise—along with its affiliates—lost more than 91 percent of its customers' funds to fees and trade-related losses.[36]

On the Inside

Thanks to the cooperation of the New York County District Attorney's Office in New York State, Committee staff interviewed Karl Spicer, an insider from Boynton Beach, Florida. Mr. Spicer worked in the retail precious metals industry for nearly seven years, most recently working for a firm indicted on charges of fraud for misleading investors. According to the District Attorney's Office, Mr. Spicer's firm, PMCO Services Inc., pressured customers to use their retirement savings to buy precious metals on leverage, taking nearly $7 million from 150 investors.[37]

According to Mr. Spicer, salespeople would typically give customers three reasons to buy precious metals,[38] emphasizing the need to act quickly to take advantage of the information. Customers were typically approached using the following setup:

> *Front Call:* An opening conversation would be used to gauge the interest and value of the customer, including an assessment of how much money the customer could be talked into investing. Interested customers were sent promotional and "educational" materials.
>
> *Closer Call:* A week later, the salesperson would call the customer to give him "new" information to prompt him to make an investment. Once a customer agreed to buy the metals, the salesperson would prep him to pass the compliance call. Usually customers were told to say "Yes" when asked if they understood all the risks involved in the transaction, which were often leveraged

transactions. Fees were also disclosed during the Closer Call, which did not follow any registered script.

Compliance Call: Once they agreed to buy the metal, customers were transferred to an operator—usually a secretary at the firm—and asked a series of questions about their understanding of the risks involved, which was recorded to comply with legal obligations. Afterward, the purchase was finalized.

Re-Up Call: Some time later the salesperson called the customer, and would indicate that he ran into the company's chief trader who had a hot tip that could benefit the customer. The customer would then be transferred to another salesperson who would pretend to be the chief trader, and who would make up a story about an impending move in the market that could lead to huge profits if acted upon quickly.

During the initial sales pitch, customers were not told of the full risk involved with the investment, or how they could end up with negative equity if they bought the metals on leverage. In fact, customers were not told of how leveraged transactions worked until after the purchase was made. According to Mr. Spicer, even though about 70 percent of the firm's customers knew what leverage was, they did not understand that they would not physically own the metal. The District Attorney's Office believes almost all of the firm's customers lost money.

VICTIMS OF DECEPTION

Throughout this investigation, Committee staff heard stories of Americans who were talked into putting their life savings into precious metals, only to later learn that they had been duped. The following is a sample of their stories:[39]

Victim 1

A Mississippi woman was convinced to spend $33,800 to buy silver but was not told 30 percent of her funds would go toward fees instead of the actual purchase of silver. She paid around $12,500 in administrative fees alone. The woman was also led to believe she wholly owned 5,000 ounces of silver, even though she only owned a marginal interest in the company's silver holdings, which vanished once the value of silver declined. Within three to four months she lost all of her money. Fortunately, with the help of the Mississippi Attorney General, the victim was able to recoup nearly $13,000.

Victim 2

Joe Melomo, a former IBM physicist who lives in Austin, Texas, received an unsolicited call from a precious metals dealer who talked him into buying gold and silver. The salesperson told him that he would realize significant profits in a very short time, claiming the price of gold would jump 50 percent in just a few weeks, and 150 percent in a few months. When the value of gold declined, he was asked by the dealer to invest more money to make up his equity loss. Unbeknownst to him, the company made all of his transactions on leverage, leading to only $3,426 of the nearly $170,000 he spent at the firm going toward the purchase of the metals. Approximately 97 percent of his funds went to fees, with an additional $37,000 charged for interest from the leveraged transactions. Neither the fees nor the interest charges were fully explained to him before the transactions were made. When Mr. Melomo finally asked the company to liquidate his holdings and give his money back, company representatives told him they couldn't because they never actually purchased any metals in his name. Instead, they pooled his money with the money of other clients in order to buy metals in the name of the company. Through a settlement agreement, he was able to recoup $25,000.

Victim 3

An 82-year-old retiree lost $52,000 when she invested in silver on leverage. She sold her personal effects and used $41,000 from her IRA annuity to buy 600 ounces of silver. Within two months, she was told she had to send in an additional $10,000 to cover the decline in value of silver. After she told the precious metals firm she didn't have the money to invest any more in silver, her account was liquidated. The firm led her to believe she could wait out any downswing in the market. Unbeknownst to her, she only owned the metal on paper, which evaporated when the value of silver suddenly declined. Eventually, the victim was able to recover about $13,000 through a settlement agreement with the company.

FEDERAL REGULATORY ACTION

Federal Trade Commission

In May 2011, the FTC issued a consumer alert about the dangers of gold fraud and published consumer education brochures.[40] Since then, the agency has gone after retail precious metal firms suspected of violating the FTC Act and the Telemarketing Sales Rule (TSR), which prohibit fraudulent or deceptive sales tactics.[41]

Under section 5(a) of the FTC Act (15 U.S.C. § 45(a)), individuals and companies are prohibited from using "unfair or deceptive acts or practices in or affecting commerce."[42] The TSR also prohibits deceptive or abusive telemarketing practices, pursuant to the Telemarketing and Consumer Fraud and Abuse Prevention Act (15 U.S.C. 6102).[43] The FTC considers violations of the TSR or the "misrepresentations or deceptive omissions of material fact" a violation of Section 5(a) of the FTC Act. TSR violators are subject to civil penalties of up to $16,000 per violation and can be required to pay restitution to injured consumers.[44] The court also has the authority to order a nationwide ban on the telemarketing activities of transgressors to prevent further violations of the law.[45]

For retail precious metal companies that make sales over the phone, the FTC considers their salespeople to be "telemarketers" engaged in telemarketing activity, pursuant to the TSR.[46] The TSR applies equally in cases where telemarketers make outbound telephone calls to "...induce the purchase of goods or services,"[47] or where the call is initiated by the consumer ". . . in response to an advertisement relating to investment opportunities."[48]

According to the FTC, it is a violation of the TSR for a telemarketer to misrepresent, *"...directly or by implication, in the sale of goods or services ... any material aspect of an investment opportunity including, but not limited to risk, liquidity, earnings potential, or profitability."*[49]

In addition to prohibiting misrepresentations, telemarketers are required to clearly and conspicuously disclose—before a customer agrees to pay for goods or services—*"the total costs to purchase, receive, or use, and the quantity of, any goods or services that are the subject of the sales offer;" and "[alll material restrictions, limitations, or conditions to purchase, receive, or use the goods or services that are the subject of the sales offer."*[50] A failure to do so is considered a "deceptive telemarketing act or practice" and a violation of the TSR.[51]

To date, the FTC has formally charged three precious metal firms, all based in Florida, with breaking the law.[52] Within the FTC's complaints against the three companies, the agency alleges the companies violated the law by:[53]

- Using high-pressure telephone sales tactics;
- Informing individuals that they would earn substantial profits in a short period of time;
- Falsely claiming there was only a minimal risk of loss with precious metal investments;
- Failing to clearly disclose all fees and commissions charged; and
- Failing to disclose that the precious metal investments were highly-leveraged and therefore risky.

The three complaints filed by the FTC allege a total of approximately $56 million in consumer losses.[54] To date, two of these cases have settled and the defendants were required to pay a combined total of $32.6 million.[55]

Commodity Futures Trading Commission

While the FTC's jurisdiction generally extends to the telemarketing practices of precious metal companies, the CFTC generally has authority over retail commodity transactions in which the commodity is not delivered within a specific period of time.[56]

The Dodd–Frank Wall Street Reform and Consumer Protection Act of 2010 expanded the CFTC's authority over retail commodity transactions.[57] Generally, for transactions in which the full price of a metal contract is not paid up front (i.e., sold on credit, margin, or leverage), retail precious metal dealers must deliver metals to their customers within 28 days of purchase or else the transaction is considered an illegal off-exchange commodity transaction.[58]

The CFTC has filed at least 22 complaints against individuals and companies that lost over $193 million of their customers' hard earned cash.[59] Of these cases, seven currently remain active.[60] The following are examples of cases the CFTC has pursued:

CFTC v. Atlantic Bullion & Coin, Inc.[61]

In 2013, the CFTC filed and settled charges against Atlantic Bullion & Coin—a South Carolina company—and its owner for operating a Ponzi scheme involving silver over an 11-year period. At least 237 investors nationwide were led to believe they purchased silver bullion, but in reality Atlantic Bullion and its owner pocketed the money without ever purchasing silver on behalf of customers. Customers were sent false account statements to hide the scheme. The defendants settled to pay $11.53 million in restitution and $23 million in civil monetary penalties. The owner was also sentenced to nearly 20 years in prison due to the fraud.[62]

In re Pan American Metals of Miami et al.[63]

In 2013, the CFTC ordered Pan American Metals of Miami and Pan American Metals of Miami Beach to pay $3.2 million in restitution and $1.5 million in civil monetary penalties for engaging in precious metals fraud. According to the CFTC, the companies sold precious metals on leverage, but failed to actually transfer ownership of the metals, disburse loan funds, or store the metals on behalf of customers. The companies also misrepresented and failed to disclose the risks associated with leveraged transactions. Over 95 percent of their customers lost money. Unfortunately, many seniors fell victim to the scheme; at least 27 percent of the combined customer base was over the age of 65.

In re Newbridge Metals, LLC[64]

In 2013, the CFTC filed and settled fraud charges against Newbridge Metals, LLC, a Florida company. Newbridge sold precious metals through leveraged transactions. Customers were told they could purchase the metals with only a 25 percent deposit, with the remainder financed through in-house credit.

However, after customers paid the deposit, they were surprised with additional costs, including a finance charge for the loan, a service charge, and a commission of 15 percent. According to the CFTC, even though Newbridge made millions of dollars from customers, they never actually bought, sold, loaned, stored, or delivered any of the metals customers paid for. The company settled, and was required to pay more than $1.5 million in restitution.

Both Newbridge and the Pan American Companies used Hunter Wise Commodities as their wholesale dealer. The CFTC filed charges against Hunter Wise in 2012, alleging it deceptively coerced customers into buying precious metals on leverage in a fraud scheme that involved 188 different precious metal companies from across the country, including Florida, California, New York, Nevada, South Carolina, and Texas. In February 2013, a district court judge issued a preliminary injunction against Hunter Wise, finding that the company provided misleading reports to customers that created the "illusion that actual commodities [were] transferred into or out of their accounts, when in reality, no real metals [were] transferred as a result of the transaction."[65]

State Regulatory Action

Even though the federal government has stepped up enforcement actions on unscrupulous retail precious metal dealers, many are able to escape oversight due to the lack of federal licensing and reporting requirements. Although many of these firms operate across state lines, state agencies are responsible for regulating the market.[66]

Since many of the precious metal firms are based in Florida, the Florida Office of Financial Regulation (OFR) has led the way in protecting consumers from the worst practices in the industry. Between 2009 and 2011, the clients and creditors of seven Florida-based precious metals businesses claimed losses of more than $54 million.[67] Working with Federal regulators, OFR helped recoup more than $10.3 million for cheated customers.[68]

OFR found that many of the firms targeted older Americans who were given misleading or conflicting information by salespeople.[69] For example, customers were led to believe they were buying physical metals when they were buying metals on leverage.[70] In reality, they were only buying an indirect ownership interest in a derivative contract that rolled-over every month and never resulted in actual delivery of the metal.[71] According to OFR, customers were also told by salespeople that the investments were low-risk, while the written documents the firm provided disclosed the high-risk nature of the investments.[72]

In addition to Florida, states like Minnesota, Texas, and North Carolina have also gotten stricter on unruly retail precious metal companies.[73] Minnesota, in particular, enacted a law to stop ex-convicts from becoming precious metal dealers.[74] A 2011 newspaper investigation found that ex-convicts and con artists—who routinely misled or defrauded customers—staffed many of the precious metal companies in the area.[75] Salesmen who had been convicted of fraud, forgery, and even bank robbery were allowed to handle the hard-earned savings of customers, totaling millions of dollars.[76]

Texas authorities have also gone after precious metal companies, many of which convince their customers—often seniors—to use their life's savings to buy coins priced at least three times their fair market value, claiming the coins would triple in value over a short period of time.[77] Meanwhile, local officials in Santa Monica, California, have pursued several coin dealers for deceiving or bullying their customers, including Goldline International, Superior Gold Group, and Merit Financial.[78] The companies were either forced to shut down or change their business practices.

In North Carolina, local officials went after a scam artist who used Craigslist to steal thousands of dollars from people interested in buying gold.[79] While the fraudster told customers they could double their money through the investments, he allegedly used the money on dinners, massages, and other personal expenses instead of gold purchases. Meanwhile, investors had no idea the man they trusted with their savings had been served with a cease and desist order from the state.[80]

COMMITTEE STAFF INTERACTION WITH FIRMS

Committee staff contacted several retail precious metal firms to learn more about common practices within the industry. The companies were selected based on a combination of factors, such as previous administrative action taken against the company or its owners, information provided to staff by state regulators, and customer complaints. Committee staff sought to find out what percentage of retail precious metal sales were made on leverage, how the firms chose salespeople, where and how the metals were acquired, the full cost of the transactions, and how the firms handled customer complaints. The companies were also asked to share their telemarketing scripts and the contracts they required customers to sign upon sale.

Very few of the firms cooperated with the Committee's investigation in good faith. After numerous calls, emails, and letters to their management and attorneys, a number of the firms used stalling tactics and offered only partial responses to the Committee staff's inquiries. On several occasions Committee staff was bounced around between company management and their attorneys, only to receive incomplete responses from some of the companies. The high degree of recalcitrance from these firms and their attorneys casts a dark shadow on their business practices and demonstrates the need to ensure that consumers are protected from misleading investment schemes.

The firms that did respond in full explained that they relied on state regulators to evaluate the qualifications of their employees. If a person obtained a telemarketing license from a state regulator, they were generally considered qualified to make sales calls—even if they had been disciplined in the past for unfair business practices by state and federal regulators. Due to this oversight, the industry has become a constant revolving door for seedy individuals looking to make a quick buck. In fact, the Committee found several instances where people who had been disciplined or scolded by the National Futures Association or state and federal regulators for questionable business practices were still operating in the industry, but under a new guise.

All of the firms alleged to have either received very few complaints or none at all the entire time they have been in business. Those that admitted to receiving customer complaints claimed they resolved the complaints through direct negotiation with the consumer. However, consumers had limited options for recourse due to mandatory arbitration clauses in their contracts. Prior to purchasing any metals, customers are required to sign a contract that typically contained a mandatory arbitration clause, under which they forfeited their right to pursue the claim in court. These mandatory arbitration clauses also put the burden on the customer to travel to the company's local jurisdiction in order to settle the dispute, making it more difficult for non-local customers to pursue their rights.

Even though the firms purportedly operated independently from each other and employed different business practices, several of them used the same sales contracts—with identical text, which suggests they at least affiliated with the same wholesale dealer. At the same time, at least one operated out of the same address and used some of the same staff as another firm that had closed after being sanctioned by a regulator.

However, the companies that were contacted differed in the amount of fees and commissions they charged. On average, the firms applied an initial charge of 7.4 percent of the metal value, in addition to a 0.5 to 1 percent monthly storage fee if the metal was allegedly stored on behalf of the customer.

The storage fee may also include an initial charge of up to $200 for opening the account. For metals purchased on leverage, an annual percentage rate (APR) was charged ranging from 7.75 to 9.5 percent. Since leveraged transactions allow retail precious metal companies to make more money from customers, several companies have relied on the product to make up a substantial part of their business. At least one firm the Committee corresponded with admitted making 70 percent of its sales through leveraged transactions.

MARKETING TO SENIORS

While some retail precious metal companies claim not to deal with seniors in any notable capacity, the CFTC has found that an overwhelming number of victims of precious metal fraud are seniors.[81] Direct observation of the companies' sales calls also suggests they employ a sophisticated method of evaluation to identify individuals with large savings. During a sales call, customers are asked about their sources of income, their age, and their assets, including how much they have in their savings and retirement accounts. If a customer falls on the low-end of the equity spectrum in terms of the amount of funds they have in their savings or retirement accounts, they are either turned away or half-heartedly pursued. While the criteria used to evaluate potential customers may not always explicitly use age as a benchmark, it does skew toward older Americans who are more likely to have a greater amount of equity built up in their retirement and savings accounts than younger Americans. This also benefits the firms by allowing them to extract a more sizeable commission.

Additionally, federal law makes it easy for precious metals to be added to individual retirement accounts (IRAs).[82] In 1981, Congress prohibited precious metals as investments in IRAs.[83] Over time, the prohibition eroded to allow IRAs to invest in coins minted by the U.S. Treasury, as well as bullion.[84] Under current law, individuals are able to purchase precious metals through an IRA on a pre-tax basis, and without having to pay an early withdrawal penalty.[85] Although the law requires any metal purchased through an IRA to be of investment grade, and not just a collectable, there are no restraints on the type of financial arrangement used to purchase the metal, such as leveraged transactions.

CONCLUSION

For too long, too many bad apples in the retail precious metals industry have been able to flout the law and cheat consumers out of millions of dollars. When precious metals became a credible alternative to the instability in the stock market in the wake of the 2008 financial crisis, questionable individuals flooded the marketplace, offering deals too good to be true.[86] What should have been an opportunity for the industry to provide financial security for the millions of Americans seeking refuge from the calamity on Wall Street, became an opportunity for dishonest individuals to run loose with high-pressure sales tactics, hidden fees, and unfair financial deals such as leveraged transactions. Committee staff conservatively estimates that more than 10,000 Americans have been victimized through these schemes, with losses around $300 million.[87]

These precious metal dealers thrived on the haze that clouds the industry in secrecy. This can be seen in the actions of the retail precious metal companies that tried to conceal their practices from the Committee staff's investigation. While some past attempts to increase transparency have proven unsuccessful,[88] some reforms—such as those contained in the Dodd-Frank Act— have led to greater oversight and insight into this ever-evolving industry.[89] Still, more may need to be done to reduce gaps in oversight and improve consumer protection.

As Americans look for new ways to achieve long-term financial security, they should be mindful of the dangers of deceitful precious metal deals. Consumer protection requires not only strong oversight by law enforcement but also an informed and educated citizenry. Fortunately, the FTC and CFTC[90] have made it a priority to educate consumers on the dangers of spurious retail precious metal dealers. Above all, consumers should be wary of any offer requiring them to "act fast."[91] As a golden rule, an investor should always take the time to closely evaluate the costs, risks, and suitability of any investment.

End Notes

[1] http://www.investopedia.com/terms/p/preciousmetal.asp

[2] https://www.fidelity

[3] Florida Office of Financial Regulation Letter to Committee Staff. (July 12, 2013)

[4] Baiocchio, Paul. The Gold ETF/Physical Gold Disconnect, (blog). April 23, 2013.

[5] Americans Choose Gold as the Best Long-Term Investment, Gallup. (August 25, 2011)

[6] Jacobe, Dennis. "Americans Choose Gold as the Best Long-Term Investment." Gallup. August 25, 2011.

[7] Jacobe, Dennis. "Gold Loses Luster in U.S. as Investment; Real Estate Gains," Gallup. April 16, 2013.

[8] Light, Joe. "What's Next for Gold." *The Wall Street Journal*. November 1, 2013.

[9] Ellin, Abby. "The Truth About Buying Gold." *ABCNews.com*. June 12, 2012.

[10] Kristof, Kathy. "Should You Invest in Gold?" *Kiplinger*. September 7, 2011.

[11] *Id.*

[12] Ellin, Abby. "The Truth About Buying Gold." *ABCNews.com*. June 12, 2012.

[13] Light, Joe. "What's Next for Gold." *The Wall Street Journal*. November 1, 2013.

[14] Florida Office of Financial Regulation Letter to Committee Staff. (July 12, 2013)

[15] *Id.*

[16] *Id.*

[17] CFTC v. Hunter Wise Commodities, LLC, et al., No. 12-cv-81311 (S.D. Fla. filed Dec. 5, 2012), pg. 10-14

[18] CFTC v. Hunter Wise Commodities, LLC, et al., No. 12-cv-81311 (S.D. Fla. filed Dec. 5, 2012), pg. 11

[19] CFTC v. Hunter Wise Commodities, LLC, et al., No. 12-cv-81311 (S.D. Fla. filed Dec. 5, 2012) and In re Pan American Metals of Miami, LLC, et al., CFTC Docket No. 13-27 (CFTC filed July 29, 2013)

[20] In re Pan American Metals of Miami, LLC, et al., CFTC Docket No. 13-27 (CFTC filed July 29, 2013) and Florida Office of Financial Regulation Letter to Committee Staff (July 12, 2013)

[21] CFTC v. Hunter Wise Commodities, LLC, et al., No. 12-cv-81311 (S.D. Fla. filed Dec. 5, 2012) ; In re Pan American Metals of Miami, LLC, et al., CFTC Docket No. 13-27 (CFTC filed July 29, 2013); CFTC v. Lions Wealth Holdings, Inc., et al., No. 2:13-cv-01787. (D. Nev. filed Sep. 30, 2013)

[22] CFTC v. Hunter Wise Commodities, LLC, et al., No. 12-cv-81311. (S.D. Fla. filed Dec. 5, 2012)

[23] Rolling spot contracts are commodity contracts meant for immediate delivery but are rolled into to the next month, moving forward the delivery date. They can be rolled forward in perpetuity. In effect, this allows traders to buy and sell the contracts without the need to ever take or make immediate delivery.

[24] CFTC v. Hunter Wise Commodities, LLC, et al., No. 12-cv-81311 (S.D. Fla. filed Dec. 5, 2012), pg. 13

[25] In re Pan American Metals of Miami, LLC, et al., CFTC Docket No. 13-27 (CFTC filed July 29, 2013), pg. 4-5 and CFTC v. Hunter Wise Commodities, LLC, et al., No. 12-cv-81311 (S.D. Fla. filed Dec. 5, 2012), pg. 10

[26] In re Pan American Metals of Miami, LLC, et al., CFTC Docket No. 13-27 (CFTC filed July 29, 2013), pg. 4-5, and CFTC v. Hunter Wise Commodities, LLC, et al., No. 12-cv-81311 (S.D. Fla. filed Dec. 5, 2012), pg. 10

[27] Florida Office of Financial Regulation Letter to Committee Staff (July 12, 2013)

[28] CFTC v. Hunter Wise Commodities, LLC, et al., No. 12-cv-81311 (S.D. Fla. filed Dec. 5, 2012), pg. 10

[29] CFTC v. Hunter Wise Commodities, LLC, et al., No. 12-cv-81311 (S.D. Fla. filed Dec. 5, 2012), pg. 11

[30] *Id.*

[31] *CFTC v. Hunter Wise Commodities,* LLC, et al., No. 12-cv-81311 (S.D. Fla. filed Dec. 5, 2012), pg. 11.

[32] Florida Office of Financial Regulation Letter to Committee Staff (July 12, 2013)

[33] $3,700 total cost, assuming $1,500 paid for a 15 percent commission, $200 paid for fees, and the loss of the original $2,000 down payment.

[34] Denina, Clara. "Gold lower, set for biggest yearly loss since 1981." *Reuters*. December 23, 2013.

[35] The Special Monitor and Corporate Manager's Initial Report for CFTC v. Hunter Wise Commodities, LLC, pg. 9

[36] The Special Monitor and Corporate Manager's Initial Report for CFTC v. Hunter Wise Commodities, LLC

[37] The People of New York v. Stropp et al. (The New York County District Attorney's Office has revised the value initially reported in the press release from nearly $8 million to nearly $7 million)

[38] Popular examples include the declining value of the dollar or the changing political environment abroad.

[39] Due to confidentiality requirements, some of the names have been withheld.

[40] "Investing in Gold." *Federal Trade Commission: Consumer Information.*

[41] FTC Stops Bogus Precious Metals Dealers; FTC Charges Bogus Precious Metals Investment Scheme; FTC Takes Action Against Bogus Precious Metals Investment Scheme

[42] U.S. Government Printing Office, *Section 5(a) of the Federal Trade Commission Act of 1914 (Public Law 63-203, 38 Stat. 717), [15 U.S.C. § 45(a)], Incorporating U.S. SAFE WEB Act amendments of 2006 (Public Law 109-455, 120 Stat. 3372).*

[43] Through the Telemarketing and Consumer Fraud and Abuse Prevention Act (15 U.S.C. § 6102), Congress directed the FTC to establish rules to prohibit deceptive or abusive telemarketing practices, causing the FTC to promulgate the TSR.

[44] "Complying with the Telemarketing Sales Rule." *Federal Trade Commission: Bureau of Consumer Protection.* (Pg. 15 of 60)

[45] U.S. Government Printing Office, *Section 13(a) of the Federal Trade Commission Act of 1914 (Public Law 63 203, 38 Stat. 717), [15 U.S.C. § 53], Incorporating U.S. SAFE WEB Act amendments of 2006 (Public Law 109-455, 120 Stat. 3372).*

[46] U.S. Government Printing Office, *Electronic Code of Federal Regulations: Title 16 §310.2(aa), (cc), and (dd).*

[47] U.S. Government Printing Office, *Electronic Code of Federal Regulations: Title 16 § 310.2(v) and (aa).*

[48] U.S. Government Printing Office, *Electronic Code of Federal Regulations: Title 16 §310.6(b)(5).*

[49] U.S. Government Printing Office, *Electronic Code of Federal Regulations: Title 16 CFR §310.3 (i) and (ii).*

[50] *Id.*

[51] U.S. Government Printing Office, *Electronic Code of Federal Regulations: Title 16 CFR §310.3*

[52] FTC Stops Bogus Precious Metals Dealers; FTC Charges Bogus Precious Metals Investment Scheme; FTC Takes Action Against Bogus Precious Metals Investment Scheme.

[53] *Id.*

[54] "FTC Stops Bogus Precious Metals Dealers." *Federal Trade Commission*; "FTC Charges Bogus Precious Metals Investment Scheme." *Federal Trade Commission*; "FTC Takes Action Against Bogus Precious Metals Investment Scheme." *Federal Trade Commission.*

[55] "FTC Action Results in $24 Million Settlement with Precious Metals Dealers." *Federal Trade Commission*; "Precious Metal Marketers Agree to Settle FTC Charges." *Federal Trade Commission*; "FTC Settlement Bans Precious Metal Marketers from Selling Investment Opportunities." *Federal Trade Commission.*

[56] CFTC Issues Interpretation Concerning Retail Commodity Transactions

[57] Miller, Rena. "The Commodity Futures Trading Commission: Background and Current Issues." Congressional Research Service. June 24, 2013 (R43117)

[58] U.S. Government Printing Office, *Section 742(a) of the Dodd-Frank Wall Street Reform and Consumer Protection Act (Public Law 111-203, 124 Stat. 1376), [7 U.S.C. § 2(c)(2)(D)].*

[59] Based on data provided by the CFTC.

[60] CFTC v. Lions Wealth Holdings, Inc., et al., No. 2:13-cv-01787 (D. Nev. filed Sep. 30, 2013); CFTC v. The Yorkshire Group Inc., et al., No. 13-5323 (E.D.N.Y. filed Sep. 25, 2013); CFTC v. AmeriFirst Management LLC, et al., No. 13-cv-61637 (S.D. Fla. filed July 29, 2013); CFTC v. Hunter Wise Commodities, LLC, et al., No. 12-cv81311 (S.D. Fla. filed Dec. 5, 2012); CFTC v. American Bullion Exchange ABEX, Corp., et al., No. 8:10-cv-01876- DOC-RNB (C.D. Cal. filed Dec. 8, 2010)

[61] CFTC v. Atlantic Bullion & Coin, Inc., et al., No. 8:12-cv-01503-JMC (D.S.C. filed Feb. 27, 2013)

[62] U.S. v. Ronnie Gene Wilson, No. 8:12-cr-00320-JMC. (D.S.C. filed April 4, 2012)

[63] In re Pan American Metals of Miami, LLC, et al., CFTC Docket No. 13-27. (CFTC filed July 29, 2013)

[64] In re Newbridge Metals, LLC, CFTC Docket No. 13-37 (CFTC filed Sep. 24, 2013)

[65] "Federal Court in Florida Enters Preliminary Injunction Order against Hunter Wise Commodities, LLC, Lloyds Commodities, LLC, and 18 Other Defendants in Connection with Operating a Multi-Million Dollar Fraudulent Precious Metals Scheme." *U.S. Commodity Futures Trading Commission*.

[66] Browning, Dan. "Minnesota May be 1st State to Regulate Retail Coin Dealers." *McClatchy News*. July 29, 2013, Florida Office of Financial Regulation Letter to Committee Staff (July 12, 2013), pg. 1-3; "Attorney General Brings Action Against AGT American Silver and Gold." Better Business Bureau – Dallas & North Texas (March 8, 2012); Ignasiak, Darrick. Alleged Internet Gold, Land Scam Results in Arrest. *The Dispatch*. October 23, 2013

[67] Burstein, Jon. "Little Regulation, Lots of Risk Can Leave Gold Investors on Shaky Ground." *Sun Sentinel*. March 19, 2011.

[68] U.S. v. Richard Eugene Engel, No. 2:10-cr-14079 (S.D. Fla. filed Oct. 7, 2010); U.S. v. Christopher Kertatos No. 2:10-cr-14079 (S.D. Fla. filed Oct. 7, 2010); U.S. v. Zito, No. 1:12-cr-20030 (S.D. Fla. filed Jan 12, 2012).

[69] Florida Office of Financial Regulation Letter to Committee Staff. (July 12, 2013)

[70] *Id.*

[71] *Id.*

[72] *Id.*

[73] Browning, Dan. Minnesota May be 1st State to Regulate Retail Coin Dealers. McClatchy News (July 29, 2013), "Attorney General Brings Action Against AGT American Silver and Gold." Better Business Bureau – Dallas & North Texas (March 8, 2012), Ignasiak, Darrick. Alleged Internet Gold, Land Scam Results in Arrest. The Dispatch (October 23, 2013)

[74] Browning, Dan. Minnesota May be 1st State to Regulate Retail Coin Dealers. McClatchy News (July 29, 2013)

[75] *Id.*

[76] Browning, Dan. Ex-cons Make a Killing in Coins. StarTribune (May 9, 2011)

[77] "Attorney General Brings Action Against AGT American Silver and Gold." *Better Business Bureau – Dallas & North Texas*. March 8, 2012. and Abbott, Greg. "All That Glitters: Investing in Gold and Rare Coins." *Weekly AG Newspaper Columns*. July 2007.

[78] Warmerdam, Elizabeth. "Santa Monica Goes After Gold & Coin Dealers." Courthouse News Service. February 18, 2014. and "Santa Monica-Based Goldline International Placed Under Injunction, Ordered To Change Sales Practices." *Santa Monica Mirror*. February 22, 2012.

[79] Ignasiak, Darrick. Alleged Internet Gold, Land Scam Results in Arrest. The Dispatch (October 23, 2013)

[80] *Id.*

[81] In re Pan American Metals of Miami, LLC, et al., CFTC Docket No. 13-27 (CFTC filed July 29, 2013)

[82] U.S. Government Printing Office, *Code of Federal Regulations, Title 26 § 408(m).* 2014

[83] U.S. Government Printing Office, *The Economic Recovery Act of 1981 (PL 97-34). 1981*

[84] U.S. Government Printing Office, *The Taxpayer Relief Act of 1997 (PL 105-34).* 1997

[85] To discourage the use of retirement funds for purposes other than normal retirement, the law generally imposes a 10 percent tax penalty on distributions from retirement accounts before the age of 59 and 6 months.

[86] Greisman, Lois. Prepared Statement of the Federal Trade Commission on the Precious Coins and Bullion Disclosure Act Before the House Energy and Commerce Committee's Subcommittee on Commerce, Trade, and Consumer Protection (September 23, 2010)

[87] Estimate based on data provided by the Commodity Futures Trading Commission ($194 million), Federal Trade Commission ($32.7 million), U.S. Department of Justice ($63.3 million), and New York County District Attorney's Office ($7 million). This does not include other state actions, including those referenced elsewhere in this document.

[88] U.S. Government Printing Office, *Coin and Precious Metal Disclosure Act (H. R. 6149).* 2010

[89] U.S. Government Printing Office, *Section 742(a) of the Dodd-Frank Wall Street Reform and Consumer Protection Act (Public Law 111-203, 124 Stat. 1376), [7 U.S.C. § 2(c)(2)(D)].*

[90] "CFTC Fraud Advisories - Precious Metals Fraud." *U.S. Commodity Futures Trading Commission.*

[91] "Investing in Bullion and Bullion Coins." *Federal Trade Commission: Consumer Information.*

In: Perils of Purchasing Precious Metals … ISBN: 978-1-62081-154-2
Editor: Giovanni Kinsey

Chapter 2

STATEMENT OF BILL NELSON, CHAIRMAN, SENATE SPECIAL COMMITTEE ON AGING. HEARING ON "EXPLORING THE PERILS OF THE PRECIOUS METALS MARKET"*

Good afternoon. Today, we're going to talk about precious metals and the schemes that have cheated Americans out of millions of dollars.

A year-long investigation by the Committee uncovered that over 10,000 Americans—many of whom are seniors—have lost nearly $300 million from these schemes.

We've all seen the commercials on TV, touting the benefits of owning precious metals, such as gold, silver, and platinum.

Indeed, many investment advisers agree that investing in precious metals can be a responsible way to diversify an investment portfolio.

But we're not here to talk about the virtues of different investment strategies. We're here to spotlight the worst practices in an industry that has run amok and largely remains in the shadows. Consumers are increasingly getting trapped in bad deals.

Some of these bad practices include charging hefty fees and commissions, using bait-and-switch tactics to sell products at highly inflated prices, using high pressure sales tactics to get consumers to buy metals on leverage, and flat out fraud.

---

* This is an edited, reformatted and augmented version of an opening statement presented April 30, 2014 before the Senate Special Committee on Aging.

Many precious metal firms will also downplay the risks associated with precious metals in order to get the customer to spend more money, which the company can raid through fees and commissions.

But the most blatant type of fraud occurs when the seller outright lies to the customer, either through a Ponzi-scheme or by charging fees for fictional services. For example, the Commodity Futures Trading Commission—testifying today—has gone after a number of companies for charging storage fees when in fact *no* metal was ever stored on the customer's behalf.

Customers can also be tricked into buying metals on credit, sometimes called "on leverage," where they're charged an interest expense on top of other fees and charges. This makes it nearly impossible for them to make money or break even. In fact, investors often end up losing money from these deals—with no metal to show for their troubles—since the company can seize the customer's holdings during a short-term dip in the market.

Clearly, wherever there's money to be made, you can bet unscrupulous individuals will soon follow. And that's what happened in this industry.

So, I look forward to hearing from our panel today, which will be able to go into greater detail about what is going on in this industry, and how law enforcement is responding to protect consumers from these schemes.

I am entering a summary of this bipartisan committee staff investigation into the record. I now yield to Senator Collins.

In: Perils of Purchasing Precious Metals … ISBN: 978-1-62081-154-2
Editor: Giovanni Kinsey

Chapter 3

Statement of Susan M. Collins, Senator, Senate Special Committee on Aging. Hearing on "Exploring the Perils of the Precious Metals Market"*

Chairman Nelson, since you and I assumed leadership of this committee, we have conducted five hearings on the various scams, swindles, and cons used by fraudsters to separate America's seniors from their hard-earned money. Today's hearing is the sixth. It is indeed a sad commentary on human nature that the cruelty of the scammers who target our nation's elderly seems limited only by their creativity -- and never by their conscience.

Today's hearing focuses on a particularly appalling scam -- the so-called "sale" of precious metals to seniors, who are eager to avoid the dangers of the stock market, trying to find a safe haven for their life savings, seeking to protect their financial independence, and wanting to pass some portion of their nest egg along to their children and grandchildren. I say so-called "sale" because, as we have discovered in our investigation, a key feature of this scam is to get the customer to pay real money for a fiction -- gold, silver, platinum, or palladium -- that the scammer never delivers, and often doesn't even own.

These scammers use dubious sales tactics to steer their victims into highly leveraged derivatives contracts where the victim acquires, not precious metal,

* This is an edited, reformatted and augmented version of an opening statement presented April 30, 2014 before the Senate Special Committee on Aging.

but a piece of paper. Too often, victims are not told they are purchasing a derivatives contract, nor are they told that leverage greatly increases the risk that they could lose their investment if the precious metal drops in value. And of course, they are not told of the exorbitant fees built into the contracts that practically guarantee they will lose money.

One company brazenly operated a Ponzi scheme that bilked 945 investors out of at least $90 million over an 11 year period, until it was shut down by federal regulators.

Over the past several years, federal and state prosecutors around the country have been pushing back against this type of fraud, and I am pleased to say they have met with some success. In preparation for this hearing, we looked at 34 federal cases involving more than 9,100 victims who lost a total of nearly 300 million dollars. As a result of federal action, many of these scammers have faced steep penalties, and some victims have been able to recover part of their financial losses.

Despite these successes, precious metals fraud remains the sixth most significant form of financial fraud in the U.S., according to a report by the Enforcement Section Committee of the North American Securities Administrators Association (NAASA). The vice-chair of that committee, Judith Shaw, is the head of the Maine Office of Securities, which I oversaw during my tenure years ago as the Commissioner of Professional and Financial Regulation. While Ms. Shaw is unable to join us in person today, she has provided written testimony which I would like to submit for the Record.

Ms. Shaw describes how con artists monitor the markets to figure out what type of scam they should run. When the stock market looks like a bad place to put your money, as it did a few years ago, fraudsters know that seniors will turn to gold and silver which they perceive as safe investments. That makes them vulnerable to precious metals scams.

Maine has been fortunate to avoid the worst of these precious metals cases, a fact Administrator Shaw attributes in part to the aggressive enforcement of Maine's Commodities law and Transient Sales law. She warns, however, that scammers may have neglected Maine due to the fact that our elderly population is less wealthy than those of other states.

There may, of course, be many good reasons to invest a portion of any well-managed, diversified portfolio in precious metals, and there are many reputable dealers who can help investors acquire those metals. Our focus today is not on legitimate dealers in precious metals, but on those who would use these metals as a tool to defraud the elderly.

Thank you, Chairman Nelson, for calling this important hearing. I look forward to hearing from our witnesses.

In: Perils of Purchasing Precious Metals … ISBN: 978-1-62081-154-2
Editor: Giovanni Kinsey

Chapter 4

STATEMENT OF ROSEMARY HOLLINGER, DEPUTY DIRECTOR OF THE DIVISION OF ENFORCEMENT, COMMODITY FUTURES TRADING COMMISSION. HEARING ON "EXPLORING THE PERILS OF THE PRECIOUS METALS MARKET"*

Good afternoon Chairman Nelson, Ranking Member Collins and members of the Committee. Thank you for the opportunity to address you today. My name is Rosemary Hollinger. I am a Deputy Director in the Division of Enforcement at the Commodity Futures Trading Commission ("CFTC" or "Commission") and I am pleased to talk about the Commission's work in regard to precious metals fraud - to be precise, off-exchange transactions in precious metals with retail customers. The Commission has been engaged in combating fraud in the precious metals area throughout my 28-year career at the Commission. And, at each point along the way, the Commission has used whatever tools it had available to combat this type of fraud. The Commission's ability to fight fraud in this area was aided in 2010, when Congress, in the Dodd–Frank Wall Street Reform and Consumer Protection Act ("Dodd-Frank"), clarified the CFTC's authority to address precious metals fraud.

Most significantly, Section 2(c)(2)(D) of the Commodity Exchange Act ("CEA" or "Act"), made sure that retail commodity transactions done on a

* This is an edited, reformatted and augmented version of a statement presented April 30, 2014 before the Senate Special Committee on Aging.

leveraged or financed basis were executed on a regulated exchange and were fully subject to the CFTC's jurisdiction. Specifically, the CFTC has jurisdiction over any agreement, contract, or transaction in any commodity that: (1) is entered into with a retail customer; (2) is entered into, or offered, on a leveraged, margined, or financed basis; (3) does not result in actual delivery within 28 days; or (4) creates an enforceable obligation to deliver between a seller and buyer in connection with the line of business of the seller and buyer. Under CEA Section 2(c)(2)(D), leveraged or financed commodity transactions with retail customers would be treated "as if" they were futures. In fraud cases, this has streamlined the Commission's efforts to bring cases against metals dealers offering financed metals while avoiding protracted battles over jurisdiction that the Commission had previously faced. In addition, Dodd-Frank also amended CEA Section 6(c)(1) making it "unlawful for any person, directly or indirectly to use or employ...in connection with...a contract of sale of any commodity in interstate commerce...any manipulative or deceptive device or deceptive device or contrivance... ." With this new provision, the Commission is able to address fraud involving precious metals that are not leveraged or financed.

Subsequent to the enactment of Dodd-Frank, the Commission has filed 21 cases utilizing these new provisions.[1] Nineteen of these cases have been filed in the area of financed precious metals pursuant to Section 2(c)(2)(D) of the CEA, and two cases were filed under Section 6(c)(1) of the CEA.

In the 19 cases filed under Section 2(c)(2)(D), the Commission charged the firms with illegally offering off-exchange leveraged or financed precious metals to retail customers, and at times with fraud. Typically, these firms operate at multiple levels. So-called metals wholesalers operate at the top of these schemes claiming to act as intermediaries between metal suppliers and retail dealers in buying and selling physical metal. The retail dealer, in turn, claims to buy and sell metals on behalf of the retail customer. In reality, the "retail dealer" is just a telemarketing firm to whom the wholesaler has outsourced its sales operations.[2]

While the Commission does not categorize its cases or keep statistics concerning the age of the victims, it has observed that senior citizens are often the victims of precious metals telemarketers and perpetrators of other types of solicitation fraud. For example, in the Commission's July 2013 action against Pan American Metals of Miami, the Commission found that the precious metals telemarketer solicited at least 46 individuals over 65 years of age, including four who are over 90 years old, one of whom was solicited while he was in hospice care.

Telemarketers fraudulently selling precious metals call their victims repeatedly to build trust and rapport and to wear down their resistance with well-rehearsed sales scripts designed to reassure their victims and close the deal. They say things such as "[w]e are bound by the law to give the best advice at all times."[3]

Once they have established trust, they often capitalize on current events or trends and say things like: "...our economy is in a recession...How long will it last? And how deep will it get?" or "The U.S. dollar is poised for new all-time lows! With almost 3 trillion new U.S. dollars being printed, it is dramatically devaluing the existing dollars in circulation."

The telemarketer then offers precious metals as an alternative. They present it as an opportunity to "...invest in the actual commodity, not just a piece of paper." They claim that this is an investment that will "protect your buying power, protect your assets and provide...the safety of gold." Gold, they point out will "always have a value." However, what is presented as "safe," "secure," and "reliable" is fraught with risk. One of those risks is that there may not be any metal, even though the telemarketer promises to "...deliver gold to your depository within 72 hours after the purchase is made." Another risk is inherent in the structure of the transactions themselves.

In the schemes the Division of Enforcement typically sees, the investment the telemarketers offer is leveraged. While they tout the benefits of compounding profits through the use of financing and leverage by pointing out that the customer can "control" more metal by using leverage, they fail to disclose that leverage also compounds risk. In fact, many of these transactions are structured in such a way so that the retail customers rarely profit and, when they do, they are encouraged to make another trade until eventually they lose their money. The transactions result in substantial fees for the metals dealers. In the typical financed transaction, significant fees are immediately paid out of the customer's initial investment.

For example, at the preliminary injunction hearing in the *Hunter Wise* litigation noted earlier, the Division presented evidence that the customers immediately incurred fees of about 38% of their initial investment. Thereafter interest and storage fees are charged every day eroding the cash value of the customer's account and increasing the likelihood of a margin call and a forced liquidation. In a typical case, when fees are taken into consideration, the price of the metal has to increase at least 25% in one year for the customer to break even. So, even if the market moves favorably, the customer can still lose money. While I cannot comment upon pending litigation, two months ago, at the hearing against Hunter Wise, the Division presented evidence that 98% of the customers closed their accounts at a loss.

The Commission continues to bring enforcement cases to stop fraud in this area. Typically, the Commission seeks to immediately freeze assets so that they will be preserved for the customers. Where assets are apparent, the Commission will ask the court to appoint a receiver to marshal the assets and make restitution to customers. In addition, the Commission will seek the imposition of civil monetary penalties and disgorgement of ill-gotten fees so that the individuals and entities do not profit from their unlawful activity.

While many CFTC metals litigations remain ongoing, since February 2013, wrongdoers in these cases have been ordered to pay more than $32 million in civil monetary penalties and more than $26 million in restitution and disgorgement. Recovery of funds in this area has been very difficult. In order to increase the deterrence effect of our cases, the Commission also works cooperatively with the Department of Justice and other federal and state criminal authorities. With the involvement of the criminal authorities, wrongdoers face the real prospect that fraudulent misconduct leads to jail time. The Commission also cooperates with federal and state regulators like the Federal Trade Commission and several state securities regulators and consumer protection boards.

Though the CFTC continues to pursue cases, as with law enforcement generally, the CFTC only has the resources to pursue a small percentage of those of which the CFTC becomes aware. Consequently, enforcement efforts must be accompanied with education of consumers about the warning signs of fraud.

For example, the CFTC publishes consumer advisories warning the public about specific unlawful activity and educates the public through its consumer outreach efforts. In January 2012, the CFTC issued a Precious Metals Consumer Fraud Advisory to alert customers to precious metals fraud.[4] The CFTC's Advisory specifically warns that companies often fail to purchase any physical metals for their customers, instead simply keeping the customers' funds. It further cautions customers that leveraged commodity transactions are unlawful unless executed on a regulated exchange. The Advisory alerts the customers of several red flags to beware of, including solicitations that: claim high profits with little risk; do not identify the bank or financial institution loaning the customer money, or fail to identify where the physical metal is located or claims that it is overseas. In addition to the Advisory, the Commission's Office of Consumer Outreach has published and promotes a Precious Metals Fraud Brochure and participates in numerous expos, makes public appearances and speeches and highlights fraud cases to the media to get the word out to the retail public.[5] The Commission relies on the public as an important source of information in carrying out its regulatory and enforcement responsibilities. Customers can report violations or other suspicious activities to our Division of Enforcement by calling 866-366-2382 or through the Commission's website, at www.cftc.gov/customerprotection/ FileaTipor Comp laint.

Again, thank you for the opportunity to appear before the Subcommittee. I will be pleased to respond to any questions you may have.

COMMODITY FUTURES TRADING COMMISSION PRECIOUS METALS ENFORCEMENT ACTIONS

Precious Metals Enforcement Actions Involving Financed Transactions

1. CFTC v. Hunter Wise Commodities, LLC, et al., No. 12-cv-81311 (S.D. Fla. filed Dec. 5, 2012) (financed; fraud; offering and entering illegal, off-exchange transactions; failure to register); see Press Release 6447-12.
2. In re Secured Precious Metals Int'l, Inc., et al., CFTC Docket No. 13-12 (CFTC filed Jan. 28, 2013) (financed; offering and entering illegal, off-exchange transactions); see Press Release 6503-13.
3. In re Barclay Metals, Inc., et al., CFTC Docket No. 13-13 (CFTC Jan. 28, 2013) (financed; offering and entering illegal, off-exchange transactions); see Press Release 6503-13.
4. In re Joseph Glenn Commodities, LLC, et al., CFTC Docket No. 13-18 (CFTC filed Mar. 27, 2013) (financed; fraud; offering and entering illegal, off-exchange transactions); see Press Release 6542-13.
5. CFTC v. Global Precious Metals, LLC, et al., No. 13-cv-21708, Default Judgment (S.D. Fla. entered Aug. 12, 2013) (financed; fraud; offering and entering illegal, off-exchange transactions); see Press Releases 6587-13 (May 13, 2013 filing), and 6670-13 (settlement).
6. CFTC v. AmeriFirst Management LLC, et al., No. 13-cv-61637 (S.D. Fla. filed July 29. 2013) (financed; fraud; offering and entering illegal, off-exchange transactions); see Press Release 6653-13.
7. In re Pan American Metals of Miami, LLC, et al., CFTC Docket No. 13-27 (CFTC filed July 29, 2013) (financed; fraud; offering and

entering illegal, off-exchange transactions); see Press Release 6653-13.

8. CFTC v. Worth Group, Inc., et al., No. 13-cv-80796 (S.D. Fla. filed Aug. 13, 2013) (financed and not financed; fraud; offering and entering illegal, off-exchange transactions); see Press Release 6666-13.
9. In re London Metals Market, LLC, et al., CFTC Docket No. 13-32 (CFTC filed Sept. 4, 2013) (financed; offering and entering illegal, off-exchange transactions); see Press Release 6680-13.
10. In re Hall, CFTC Docket No. 13-32 (CFTC filed Sept. 4, 2013) (financed; offering and entering illegal, off-exchange transactions); see Press Release 6681-13.
11. In re Newbridge Metals, LLC, CFTC Docket No. 13-37 (CFTC filed Sept. 24, 2013) (financed; offering and entering illegal, off-exchange transactions); see Press Release 6705-13.
12. CFTC v. The Yorkshire Group Inc., et al., No. CV 13-5323 (E.D.N.Y. filed Sep. 25, 2013) (financed; offering and entering illegal, off-exchange transactions); see Press Release 6713-13.
13. CFTC v. Lions Wealth Holdings, Inc., et al., No. 2:13-cv-01787 (D. Nev. filed Sep. 30, 2013) (financed; fraud; offering and entering illegal, off-exchange transactions); see Press Release 6729-13.
14. CFTC v. Vertical Integration Group LLC, et al., No. 9:14-cv-80038 (S.D. Fla. filed Jan. 13, 2014) (financed; offering and entering illegal, off-exchange transactions); see Press Release 6824-14.
15. In re Worth Asset Mgt. LLC, et al., CFTC Docket No. 14-07 (CFTC filed Feb. 18, 2014) (financed; fraud; offering and entering illegal, off-exchange transactions); see Press Release 6859-14.
16. CFTC v. Gold Distributors Inc., et al., CFTC Docket No. 0:14-cv-60695 (S.D. Fla. filed Mar. 19, 2014) (financed; offering and entering illegal, off-exchange transactions); see Press Release 6884-14.
17. In re PGS Capital Wealth Mgt., et al., CFTC Docket No. 14-14 (CFTC filed Apr. 7, 2014) (financed; offering and entering illegal, off-exchange transactions); see Press Release 6909-14.
18. In re Rockwell Asset Mgt., Inc., et al., CFTC Docket No. 14-13 (CFTC filed Apr. 7, 2014) (financed; offering and entering illegal, off-exchange transactions); see Press Release 6909-14.
19. In re Empire Sterling Metals Corp., et al., CFTC Docket No. 14-15 (CFTC filed Apr. 17, 2014) (financed; offering and entering illegal, off-exchange transactions); see Press Release 6912-14.

Other Precious Metals Enforcement Actions

1. CFTC v. Atlantic Bullion & Coin, Inc. et al., No. 8:12-cv-01503-JMC (D.S.C. filed June 6, 2012, settled Feb. 27, 2013) (not financed, fraud); see Press Releases 6275-12 (filing), 6524-13 (settlement).
2. CFTC v. Smithers, No. 9:12-cv-81165-KAM, Default Judgment (S.D. Fla. entered July 31, 2013) (not financed; fraud; violation of prior Commission order); see Press Releases 6397-12 (filing on Oct. 22, 2012), and 6659-13 (default judgment).

End Notes

[1] The Commission most often learns of these matters through direct customer complaints to the CFTC and through referrals from federal and state agencies.

[2] The two cases filed under Section 6(c)(1) alleged fraudulent sales where there was no underlying metal.

[3] The examples of solicitation practices are from evidence presented by the Division of Enforcement at a preliminary injunction hearing in the Commission's pending litigation against Hunter Wise Commodities, LLC, et al., No. 12-CV-81311 (S.D. Fla. filed Dec. 5, 2012) ("Hunter Wise"). The Division successfully obtained the preliminary injunction, the issuance of which was affirmed on appeal by the United States Court of Appeals for the Eleventh Circuit, No. 13-10993 (11th Cir. Apr. 15, 2014) (the court of appeals also found the Commission had enforcement authority over leveraged or financed precious metals retail commodity transactions pursuant to Section 2(c)(2)(D)).

[4] Commodity Futures Trading Commission, Precious Metals Consumer Advisory, available at http://www.cftc.gov/ConsumerProtection/FraudAwarenessPrevention/CFTCFraudAdvisorie s/frau dadv preciousmetals.

[5] Commodity Futures Trading Commission, Precious Metals Fraud Brochure, available at http://www.cftc.gov/consumerprotection/resource.

In: Perils of Purchasing Precious Metals … ISBN: 978-1-62081-154-2
Editor: Giovanni Kinsey

Chapter 5

STATEMENT OF DAMA BROWN, DIRECTOR, SOUTHWEST REGION, FEDERAL TRADE COMMISSION. HEARING ON "EXPLORING THE PERILS OF THE PRECIOUS METALS MARKET"*

1. INTRODUCTION

Chairman Nelson, Ranking Member Collins, and Members of the Committee, I am Dama Brown, Director of the Southwest Region of the Federal Trade Commission ("FTC" or "Commission"). I appreciate the opportunity to testify today about scams arising from the sale of precious metals investments.[1] Although precious metals can be legitimate and valuable investments, some fraudsters have used them to swindle money from consumers. These scams often prey on older Americans concerned about the security of their retirement savings, particularly during periods of economic uncertainty.

Following the economic downturn in 2008, the Commission observed a proliferation of schemes targeting financially-distressed consumers.[2] These schemes have included deceptive telemarketing operators posing as "brokers" and offering precious metals as purported high-profit, low-risk investments. By failing to disclose key information about the investments' terms and high

* This is an edited, reformatted and augmented version of a statement presented April 30, 2014 before the Senate Special Committee on Aging.

costs, these brokers deceive consumers into believing that the investments provide a safe and secure vehicle for savings. Sadly, many Americans have lost their life savings to these unscrupulous operations.

Today's testimony will describe precious metals scams, the Commission's enforcement actions to stop them, and the agency's efforts to educate consumers on how to avoid them.

2. Precious Metals

Precious metals are naturally-occurring metals that carry a high economic value, often due to scarcity or global demand. These metals, including gold, silver, platinum, and palladium, can be sold as physical assets, in the form of bars, bullion, or coins, or as futures contracts or other speculative investments. Although precious metals prices are volatile, they have increased markedly over the last decade.[3] These gains occurred during a time of turbulence for more traditional investment products, including stocks, bonds, and real estate. Throughout this period, financial reports and media headlines frequently touted the significant gains in value that precious metals were experiencing contrasted against poor yields in other investments.

Fraudsters have used this backdrop to lure consumers into purchasing bogus precious metals investments. Beginning in 2010, the Commission observed an increase in investment-related frauds, including precious metals scams.[4] This increase was similar to one the Commission observed in the 1980-90s, another time when American consumers lost confidence in traditional investments and turned to alternative investment products like precious metals.[5]

3. The Commission's Law Enforcement Actions

The Commission has recently filed three law enforcement actions involving precious metals investment schemes.[6] In addition to stopping the alleged scams, the Commission expects to return approximately $5 million to consumer victims. As alleged in the Commission's complaints in these matters, the defendants' conduct followed a similar pattern. Therefore, this testimony first describes some common features of these schemes, and then provides details from each of our individual actions.[7]

A. Common Features of Precious Metals Schemes

In its enforcement actions, the Commission alleged that the scams were initiated by unsolicited telemarketing calls to consumers from a purported precious metals broker. The telemarketers often claimed to have insider information or falsely implied that the consumers were receiving a special opportunity to invest in a program ordinarily only available to investors with multi-million dollar investment portfolios. Citing recent media reports concerning the economy or precious metals performance, the telemarketers worked to convince consumers that they were offering a safe and lucrative investment opportunity in precious metals.

According to the Commission's complaints, the sales pitches used by these telemarketers contained numerous claims that the offered precious metals—which were purportedly in the form of bars, bullion, or coins—were certain to rise in price. They distinguished the telemarketers' precious metals investments from futures, options, or other "risky transactions," and explained that because the investment was backed by physical metal, the investment was safe and consumers would not lose money.[8] Telemarketers used the actual market performance of precious metals in their sale presentations: When prices rose, they urged consumers to invest quickly before prices rose further. When prices were low, they asserted that "now is the time to buy"—before prices increased. They also used aggressive sales techniques, often calling consumers for weeks, to pressure them into investing.

As alleged by the Commission, in reality, the telemarketers offered a highly leveraged, high-risk investment. With these leveraged investments, consumers paid only a portion of the purchase price and financed the remainder. The telemarketers failed to disclose this crucial information, simply claiming instead that consumers needed to pay only a percentage of the purchase price—generally 20-25 percent. They assured consumers that the balance of the purchase price would be paid from increases in equity that they claimed would be realized as precious metals prices soared. However, the Commission alleged that the telemarketers failed to disclose that their firms would charge interest, ranging from 7 to 14 percent per annum, on the 75-80 percent of the purchase price that was financed. Likewise, the telemarketers failed to clearly disclose their commission and fees, which included a 15 percent commission on the full purchase price (including the amount that was leveraged), a $200 account opening fee, monthly storage or maintenance fees, and mark ups. In addition, they failed to explain that the transaction was subject to equity calls or forced liquidation upon a price decrease.

4. Consumer Education

The Commission has produced several educational brochures to help consumers avoid scams and understand the key information they need to know before investing in precious metals, coins, or other investments.[14] For example, the *Investing in Gold*[15] brochure advises consumers to purchase gold investments only from licensed commodity brokers and reminds them that gold prices can fluctuate.

The Commission's *Investing in Bullion and Bullion Coins*[16] and *Investing in Collectible Coins*[17] materials explain the differences between bullion, bullion coins, and historic coins. While the value of bullion and bullion coins is determined by their precious metals content, the value of historic coins depends upon their historical or aesthetic value to collectors, as well as their rarity or condition. Accordingly, the precious metals value of a historic coin may be greater or less than its value as a collectible.

The FTC provides further practical investment advice in *Investing Online*,[18] *Investment Risks*,[19] and *Investment and Biz Opp Seminars*[20] publications. Among the useful tips, these publications caution consumers to be skeptical about "success stories" and to carefully research both the offered investment and the firm offering the investment.

Conclusion

Thank you for providing the Commission this opportunity to appear before the Committee to discuss the important consumer protection issues arising from precious metals investment scams. The Commission remains committed to protecting consumers from deceptive or unfair practices and appreciates the Committee's interest in this subject.

End Notes

[1] This written statement represents the views of the Commission. My oral presentation and responses to questions are my own, and do not necessarily represent the views of the Commission or any individual Commissioner.

[2] Since 2008, the Commission has brought more than 100 enforcement actions against defendants seeking to take advantage of economically vulnerable consumers. The FTC has worked closely with other federal and state agencies in coordinated sweeps, which have resulted in over 400 additional actions. See, e.g., Press Release, FTC Cracks Down on Scammers

Trying to Take Advantage of the Economic Downturn (July 1, 2009), available at http://ftc.gov/opa/2009/07/shortchange.shtm; Press Release, FTC Cracks Down on Con Artists Who Target Jobless Americans (Feb. 17, 2010), available at http://www.ftc.gov/opa/2010/02/bottondollar.shtm.

[3] For example, between 2003 and 2012, gold trading prices increased from approximately $340 per ounce to more than $1,650 per ounce, peaking at around $1,900 per ounce in September 2011. In 2013, gold prices declined sharply, closing the year around $1,200 per ounce. See Kitco Historical Charts – Gold 2000, available at http://www.kitco.com/scripts/hist charts/yearly graphs.plx.

[4] While precious metals frauds have never been one of the top complaints received by the Commission, we documented an increase in investment-related complaints and complaints involving precious metals between 2009 and 2012. See 2013 Consumer Sentinel Network Report, available at http://www.ftc.gov/enforcement/consumer-sentinel-network/reports.

[5] Following the 1970s recession, consumers were lured into alternative investments, including oil and gas leases, fine art, gemstones, and precious metals. The Commission responded with dozens of enforcement actions against companies offering bogus investments and returned tens of millions of dollars to injured consumers. See Prepared Statement of the Federal Trade Commission, "The Precious Coins and Bullion Disclosure Act," Before the Subcommittee on Commerce, Trade, and Consumer Protection of the House Committee on Energy and Commerce, 111th Cong., Sept. 23, 2010, available at http://democrats. energy commerce.house.gov/documents/20100923/ctcp/Greisman.Testimony.09.23.2010.pdf.

[6] FTC v. American Precious Metals, LLC, Civ. No. 0-11-cv-61072-WJZ (S.D. Fla. Nov. 19, 2012) (stipulated final judgment); FTC v. Premier Precious Metals, Inc., Civ. No. 12-cv-60504- RNS (S.D. Fla. Feb. 25, 2014) (stipulated final judgment); and FTC v Sterling Precious Metals, LLC, Civ. No. 12-cv-80597-KAM (S.D. Fla. Feb. 25, 2014) (stipulated final judgment).

[7] The evidence gathered to support the Commission's complaint allegations in each matter included declarations from injured consumers, the defendants' telemarketing scripts, and post-sale audio recordings made by the defendants.

[8] For example, in the American Precious Metals case, supra Note 6, consumers reported that the defendants assured them that metals prices were "poised to skyrocket" and would cause consumers' investments to quickly double or triple in value. Telemarketers also described the investment as a "safe haven." The consumers' testimony was corroborated by the defendants' own telemarketing scripts.

[9] 15 U.S.C. § 45(a) and 16 C.F.R. Part 310.3 et seq., respectively.

[10] Press releases and key pleadings concerning this action are available at http://www.ftc.gov/enforcement/cases-proceedings/102-3212/american-precious-metals-llc-et-al.

[11] The individual defendant and owner of the Premier Precious Metals companies had previously worked at American Precious Metals, LLC.

[12] Press releases and key pleadings concerning this action are available at http://www.ftc.gov/enforcement/cases-proceedings/122-3009/premier-precious-metals-inc-et-al.

[13] The press releases and key pleadings concerning this action are available at http://www.ftc.gov/enforcement/cases-proceedings/1223027/sterling-precious-metals-llc-et-al.

[14] The Commission's investment-related materials can be found at http://www.consumer.ftc.gov/topics/investments-grants.

[15] Available at http://www.consumer.ftc.gov/articles/0134-investing-gold.

[16] Available at http://www.consumer.ftc.gov/articles/0135-investing-bullion-and-bullion-coins.

[17] Available at http://www.consumer.ftc.gov/articles/0136-investing-collectible-coins.
[18] Available at http://www.consumer.ftc.gov/articles/0021-investing-online.
[19] Available at http://www.consumer.ftc.gov/articles/0238-investment-risks.
[20] Available at http://www.consumer.ftc.gov/articles/0239-investment-biz-opp-seminars.

In: Perils of Purchasing Precious Metals ... ISBN: 978-1-62081-154-2
Editor: Giovanni Kinsey

Chapter 6

TESTIMONY OF KARL SPICER, FORMER PRECIOUS METALS TELEMARKETER. HEARING ON "EXPLORING THE PERILS OF THE PRECIOUS METALS MARKET"*

Thank you Chairman Nelson, Ranking Member Collins, and distinguished members of the Special Committee on Aging for this opportunity to testify at this important hearing on the protection of the elderly.

My name is Karl Spicer and, as a result of my participation in a South Florida- based commodities fraud scheme, I am a convicted felon. Consequently, I have firsthand knowledge of the deceptive methods employed by scam artists to entice unsuspecting and vulnerable victims to part with their hard earned savings in fraudulent "investment opportunities."

As this Special Committee is uniquely aware, because of their accumulated assets, the elderly are particularly attractive targets for a wide array of fraudsters, regardless of the specific nature of the investment vehicle being offered to the public. From my vantage point, it is clear that the elderly need to be well-educated and equipped with the necessary skills to protect themselves from financial exploitation.

My purpose in testifying today is to provide the Special Committee with some measure of insight into the specific methods used by trained salesmen to deceive the investing public. I wish to impress upon the Special Committee that my willingness to speak candidly about the so called "tools of the trade" is

* This is an edited, reformatted and augmented version of testimony presented April 30, 2014 before the Senate Special Committee on Aging.

based upon a clear recognition of the magnitude of the monetary and emotional harm that my conduct has caused to the victims in my specific case. The recognition of the harm that I caused is further compounded by the realty that, in all likelihood, I will never be able to provide the victims with any appreciable measure of relief. It is my hope that, by testifying about the pitfalls in succumbing to "high pressure" sales tactics, I can help prevent elderly victims from being ensnared in ongoing or new investment scams. I wish to invite the Special Committee to probe my knowledge of the tactics employed in such scams and to specifically delve into the nature and degree of my conduct in the specific scheme for which I stand convicted.[1]

Briefly, by way of background, I am thirty-seven years old and I was born in Beckley, West Virginia. My younger sister and I were raised by our mother, a single mom who was employed in the health care industry. In 1994, when I was eighteen, our family moved to South Florida so that my mother could take advantage of a new employment opportunity. Because of the long hours required by my mother's new position, I raised my younger sister during the years she attended middle school. My sister eventually attained her law degree at a prestigious university and is now a practicing attorney.

In approximately 2000, after working a number of years in the construction industry, I became a licensed commodities broker in South Florida. After cycling through a number of questionable firms, some of which came under the scrutiny of the Commodities Futures Trading Commission, I became steeped in the methods used to sell investment opportunities, as well as the techniques employed to offset investor efforts to delay or avoid investment commitments. Throughout the period of time that I was a commodities broker in South Florida I earned commissions in the approximate amount of $1,500,000.

Eventually, in about March 2012, I became affiliated with a with a South Florida commodities firm known as PMCO Services, Inc. From that period of time through February 2013, myself and a number of business associates engaged in a systematic scheme to defraud the investing public through the sale of silver bullion and other precious metals through PMCO. The PMCO scheme involved 150 harmed investors and resulted in approximately $7,000,000 in losses. As a result of my effort, I earned approximately $227,000 in commissions from the PMCO scheme. Throughout this time-period, my conduct and that of my business associates was intended to defraud investors who purchased precious metals through the company.

In essence, PMCO salesmen were pitching clients on an opportunity to invest in a "Leveraged Program" for the purported purchase of precious metals. The allure of a leveraged program is specifically designed to entice clients by offering the ability to finance a significant portion of the investment. Consequently, in addition to paying an up-front portion of the investment in the program, investors were also charged finance fees. These fees were not adequately explained to potential clients. Moreover, due to fluctuations in the commodities market, investors could be subject to margin calls which could result in the sale of their existing position or in the payment of additional funds to off-set a deficiency in their account.

As an "introducing broker" in the sale of commodities, PMCO purchased leads from a number of sources, including vendors who regularly secured identifying information from other telemarketing firms or "boiler rooms." As an introducing firm, PMCO secured an affiliation with an entity known as AmeriFirst Inc., a "clearing firm," which was required to effectuate the trades and to also ensure the storage of the specific metals that were purportedly purchased by the investor.

In general, after identifying viable candidates from the lead list, a "fronter," a less experienced salesman, would utilize a devised sales "script" and contact a potential investor in order to gauge potential interest, including an initial assessment of the amount of money the customer could be enticed to committing to the metals program. The fronter would immediately forward to an interested customer a glossy promotional package. Shortly thereafter, a salesman, known as a "closer," would follow up with the potential investor and impart "new" information which was designed to insure an investment in the metals program. In order to construct a superficial layer of plausible deniability, the new client was directed to the "Compliance Department," in realty an untrained secretary or other administrative person. The closer would "school" the investor to give appropriate responses during the recorded compliance call, including a confirmation that the client was specifically aware of the risks associated with the highly speculative nature of the leveraged program.

As with any investment scam and in order to effectuate the goals and objectives of the scheme, my associates and I deliberately deceived investors by making a number of affirmative misrepresentations and by also failing to disclose material facts concerning the investment opportunity.

More specifically, we intentionally deceived potential investors into believing that PMCO was a well-established firm located in the financial district in New York City, when in fact the company was located in South Florida. In addition, administrative personal were also directed to inform

In: Perils of Purchasing Precious Metals … ISBN: 978-1-62081-154-2
Editor: Giovanni Kinsey

Chapter 7

TESTIMONY OF JOE MELOMO, FORMER IBM PHYSICIST. HEARING ON "EXPLORING THE PERILS OF THE PRECIOUS METALS MARKET"*

Chairman Nelson, Ranking Member Collins, and other members of the Committee,

My name is Joe Melomo. I have had considerable success in my business life as a former physicist for IBM. My wife and I have raised 4 successful children, of whom I am very proud. I was raised to always try to do the right thing and to treat other people the way I would like to be treated. I consider myself a savvy businessman and investor, and yet I sit here today having lost more than $170,000 investing in what I know now was a precious metal scam.

So that you can understand my frame of mind at the time I invested in precious metals, I would like to share with you events leading up to the call I received from American Precious Metals. My wife passed away at the end of 2001 after 41 years of marriage and I was lost, and found it very hard to look back. I sold my house in 2004 and moved from the outskirts of Austin to downtown Austin to be closer to my children and grandchildren.

In Austin, after much due diligence, I became a silent partner in a restaurant but soon discovered the majority partner in the business was stealing money. While I succeeded in proving this in court – the man was

* This is an edited, reformatted and augmented version of testimony presented April 30, 2014 before the Senate Special Committee on Aging.

convicted of fraud – he was unable to pay me the $250,000 the court ordered him to pay me. So, at age 71, I took over the business, dealing with all the stress that comes with having to support a team of employees and their families, and cover the enormous bills that came due.

While this was all going on I received a call from American Precious Metals, even though my number was on the "Do not call registry." The person who called talked to me about investing in precious metals, primarily gold and silver. The conversation got my attention because I could see a way to possibly cover some of my losses from the restaurant. So I asked him to send me some information, which he did. All of the materials looked very professional and legitimate. Between his encouragement and what seemed to be genuine interest in helping me profit from this kind of investment, and my desire to make back some money, I started to invest in gold and silver.

I never truly understood the leveraged process, and was not clear on the kind of fees I would be charged. Storage, commission and interest fees were never discussed. I trusted him to watch out for my interests since I explained to him the kind of turmoil I was going through at the restaurant. He told me there is some risk associated with precious metal investments, but assured me that he would be watching out for me. I guess that feeling of assurance allowed me to let my guard down. So with that I focused my attention on trying to correct all the issues with the restaurant. When the monthly statements came I looked at them, but I didn't really understand them. All I did make of them was my investment was looking good. Occasionally, I would call asking if I should be concerned about my investment and was told no and that it still looked good.

During this period, several different sales representatives worked my account. The sales representative working with me changed for various reasons. But each salesperson that was assigned to me made me feel like I was a friend. We talked about our children, and where we went to school.

For almost an entire year they kept calling me and urging me to invest more money because everything looked good.

Around August 2008 the precious metals prices dropped significantly and most of my precious metals were liquidated. American Precious Metals contacted me and told me to send more money to protect my investment. I told them I didn't have any more and that I wanted them to return my money. They said they didn't have it. I called numerous times demanding that they return my money and then ultimately they said it was entirely gone. I was devastated to realize that I had been deceived by this company. I paid American Precious Metals just under $170,000 and they charged me approximately $165,000 in administrative fees and $37,000 in interest charges. With the help of an attorney, I was able to only get back $25,000. The overall loss from this investment, along with the cost of the restaurant, completely depleted my retirement savings.

When I told my children what had happened, they were extremely upset with me and with American Precious Metals.

My daughter Nancy took it upon herself to research the company and the people who worked there. She found that they were banned once before for doing the exact same thing, but they restarted under a different name. She contacted the Federal Trade Commission and specifically Ms. Dama Brown. Between my daughter's tenacious drive and the excellent work by Ms. Brown and the FTC staff, they were able to get the people from American Precious Metals convicted in December 2012.

I commend Ms. Dama Brown and her staff at the FTC for following through and getting this conviction. Unfortunately, to this day I still have not fully recovered the money that I lost to American Precious Metals.

I come here today to have my story serve as a warning to others who may fall victim to this trap, and encourage our elected leaders to help protect us little guys from the predatory schemes of these companies. I thank you for the opportunity to share my story, and stand ready to answer any questions.

Thank you,
Joe Melomo

In: Perils of Purchasing Precious Metals … ISBN: 978-1-62081-154-2
Editor: Giovanni Kinsey

Chapter 8

INVESTING IN BULLION AND BULLION COINS*

Federal Trade Commission

If you're thinking about investing in bullion or bullion coins, the Federal Trade Commission (FTC), the nation's consumer protection agency, says your best bet is to research your options and get smart. Being uninformed can have serious consequences.

Bullion is a bulk quantity of precious metal, usually gold or silver, assessed by weight, typically cast as ingots or bars, and sold by major banks and dealers. You also can buy bullion as coins.

Bullion coins are minted from precious metal, usually gold or silver, and bought for investment purposes from major banks, coin dealers, brokerage firms, and precious metal dealers. Their value is based on their gold or silver bullion content. Prices fluctuate daily, depending on the price of gold and silver in the world markets. Perhaps the best-known bullion coins are the American Gold Eagle, the Canadian Maple Leaf, the Australian Gold Nugget, and the South African Krugerrand.

The U.S. Mint has produced gold, silver and platinum bullion coins since 1986, and guarantees their precious metal content. The Mint produces two types of bullion coins:

---

* This is an edited, reformatted and augmented version of an article provided on the following FTC website: http://www.consumer.ftc.gov/articles/0135-investing-bullion-and-bullion-coins (viewed June 2014).

- *Proof bullion coins*, which are specially minted for collectors and usually sold in a protective display case directly by the Mint.
- *Uncirculated bullion coins*, which are minted for investment purposes and sold to a select number of authorized buyers based on the current market price (the spot price) for the precious metal plus a small premium charged by the Mint.

Foreign governments also mint coins, but they may not be produced to the same standards as U.S. coins and they aren't guaranteed by the U.S. government. The value of foreign bullion coins depends primarily upon the coin's melt value – the basic intrinsic bullion value of a coin if it were melted and sold. A bullion coin's condition – its "grade" – isn't the most relevant factor in determining its price.

INVESTIGATE BEFORE YOU INVEST

Investing in bullion or bullion coins is a big decision. If you're thinking about it:

- Ask for the coin's melt value. The melt value for virtually all bullion coins and collectible coins is widely available.
- Consult with a reputable financial advisor you trust who has specialized investment knowledge. You may want to talk to other investors, too.
- Shop around. Most banks offer gold bullion, often at a lower markup than dealers. You also can enter the name of the coin into an online search engine to compare prices from other dealers.
- Get an independent appraisal of the specific asset you're considering. The seller's appraisal might be inflated.
- Consider additional costs associated with the investment. You may need to buy insurance or a safe deposit box, or you may need to rent offsite storage to safeguard your bullion. These costs will cut into the investment potential of bullion.
- Be wary of buying bullion or bars that won't be delivered to you, but rather to a "secured facility," by the seller or a third party. When you buy metals without taking delivery, you face the risk that the metal doesn't exist, isn't of the quality described, or isn't properly insured.

- Walk away from sales pitches that minimize risk and sales representatives who claim that written risk disclosures are just formalities required by the government, and therefore not necessary. Reputable sales reps are upfront about the risk of particular investments.
- Refuse to "act now," regardless of the consequences. Any sales pitch that urges you to buy immediately is a signal to walk away and keep your money in your pocket.
- Check out the company by entering its name in a search engine online. Read whether other people have something to say about their experiences with the company. Try to communicate offline if possible to clarify any details. In addition, contact your state Attorney General (www.naa.org) and local consumer protection agency (www.usa.gov/directory/stateconsumer/index.shtml). Checking with these organizations in the communities where promoters are located is a good idea, but realize that it isn't fool-proof: it just may be too soon for someone to realize they've been defrauded or to have lodged a complaint with the authorities.
- Ask for a guarantee or certificate of authenticity for the bullion's precious metal content. Research the company behind the guarantee or certificate because certificates of 'authenticity' can be faked.

TIP-OFFS TO RIP-OFFS

Bullion scams often involve false claims about content, rarity or value:

False Claims – Unscrupulous sellers often overprice their coins, lie about the bullion content, or try to pass off ordinary bullion coins as rare collectible coins. Some fraudulent dealers may even try to sell coins that aren't bullion coins at all. Others may try to sell bullion pieces with the same design as coins from the U.S. Mint, but in different sizes. Indeed, private mints issue coins that look like bullion coins minted by foreign governments, but may have little or no gold content. Your best defense is to study the market and choose your dealer carefully.

Leveraged Investment Scams – Leveraged investments are high-risk investments that can result in the loss of even more money than you originally invested. Typically, in a leveraged investment scam, a telemarketer or website will state that the price of metal is about to skyrocket and that you can make significant profits by making a small down payment for the metal, often as low as 20 percent. According to the marketer, by paying only 20 percent of the purchase price, you can get more metal than if you had to pay 100 percent of the purchase price.

In reality, you have borrowed money – as much as 80 percent of the purchase price of the metal – from a financial institution that claims it will hold the metal for you, and charge you monthly storage fees and interest charges. Rather than sending you a bill for those fees, the institution will reduce your equity in the investment. Once your equity falls below a certain level (for example, 15 percent of the purchase price), the financial institution will issue an "equity call," requiring you to pay additional money to bring your equity above the equity call level. If you can't pay or refuse to pay additional money, the lender will sell the metal to pay off your loan and send you a bill if the sale of the metal does not cover the amount you owe.

These investments are high-risk because you will receive an equity call if the price of the metal goes down, stays flat, or simply doesn't go up enough to offset the mounting storage and interest charges.

Glossary of Gold

Ask Price – The selling price a dealer offers.

Bid Price – The price a dealer pays for bullion or coins.

Bullion – Precious metals like platinum, gold or silver in the form of bars or other storage shapes. Bullion coins are made of these metals, too.

Collector Coin, Historic Coin, or Numismatic Coin – A coin whose value is based on rarity, demand, condition, and mintage; in fact, it may be worth more than its bullion value.

Melt Value – The basic intrinsic bullion value of a coin if it were melted and sold.

Premium – The amount by which the market value of a gold coin or bar exceeds the actual value of its gold content. The seller can recover part of the premium at resale.

Spot Price – The current price in the physical market for immediate delivery of gold; sometimes called the cash price.

Spread – The difference between the buying price and the selling price.

Troy Ounce – The unit of weight for precious metals. One troy ounce equals 480 grains, 1.09711 ounces, or 31.103 grams.

For More Information

Check these websites for additional information:

- Commodity Futures Trading Commission – cftc.gov
- U.S. Mint – usmint.gov
- U.S. Securities and Exchange Commission – sec.gov and investor.gov
- American Numismatic Association – money.org
- National Futures Association – nfa.futures.org
- World Gold Council – gold.org

In: Perils of Purchasing Precious Metals ... ISBN: 978-1-62081-154-2
Editor: Giovanni Kinsey

Chapter 9

INVESTING IN COLLECTIBLE COINS*

Federal Trade Commission

If you're thinking about buying collectible coins as an investment, the Federal Trade Commission (FTC), the nation's consumer protection agency, has three words for you: research, research, research. In fact, the agency says, there isn't a potential investor around who can afford not to spend time researching the coins, the graders who assess them, and the dealers who sell them.

Collectible coins have some historic or aesthetic value to collectors. The value of many collectible coins exceeds their melt value because their precious metal content is so small. Coin collectors refer to this collectible value as numismatic value, and they say it is determined by factors like the type of coin, the year it was minted, the place it was minted, and its condition – or "grade."

Dealers who sell collectible coins often have valuable coins graded by professional services. A grader examines the coin's condition based on a set of criteria. Then the grader assigns it a numerical grade from one to 70, and places it in a plastic cover for protection. But factors like "overall appearance" and "eye appeal" are subjective, and the grade assigned to a particular coin can vary among dealers. What's more, fine distinctions between grades can mean big differences in the value or price of a coin. The difference of one grade in

* This is an edited, reformatted and augmented version of an article provided on the following FTC website: http://www.consumer.ftc.gov/articles/0136-investing-collectible-coins (viewed June 2014).

the same coin can mean the loss or gain of thousands of dollars in value. Subjectivity in grading means there is real inherent risk in coin investing.

Expect to hold your investment for at least 10 years before possibly realizing a profit. That's because dealers usually sell collectible coins at a markup. It's how they make their money. In addition, the market for numismatic coins may not be the same as the market for precious metals or bullion coins. It's possible that the price of gold can increase while the value of a numismatic coin decreases.

Investigate Before You Invest

If you're thinking of investing in collectible coins, take your time and get to know the subject.

- Ask for the coin's melt value – the basic intrinsic bullion value of a coin if it were melted and sold. The melt value for virtually all bullion coins and collectible coins is widely available.
- Read trade magazines to check the wholesale value of coins. Keep in mind that collectible coins generally sell for a premium or markup over the wholesale price so the dealer can make a profit. You can find up-to-date wholesale value listings in trade magazines, like the Coin Dealer Newsletter and Certified Coin Dealer Newsletter.
- Be clear on the commission or fees that the metals dealer or broker is charging.
- Examine coins in person. It's difficult, if not impossible, to make a practical decision about buying a particular coin based on a photo or a conversation with the seller.
- Ask about the coin's grade. If the coin has been professionally graded, check into the grading service. Is it independent from the dealer? What's its reputation in the industry? Two services commonly used by dealers are Professional Coin Grading Service (PCGS) and Numismatic Guaranty Corporation (NGC). If you suspect that a coin's grade is fake or has been modified, check out the serial number on the coin's case or the grading document. Most legitimate graders assign a serial number to each coin they grade so buyers can verify the grade independently. You can check the serial number online or on the phone.

- Get a second opinion about the grade and value of the coin you're considering as a double-check on the validity of the grade.
- Get a written copy of the return policy. Many reputable dealers offer a return period if you're not satisfied with your purchase. Fourteen days is typical.
- Ask about buy-back policies because they vary among dealers. Some may offer to buy back your coin if its condition is the same as when you bought it from them. Others will buy your coin, but charge you a commission fee. Still others may offer only a store credit.
- Consider the tax implications. The Internal Revenue Service classifies certain gold products as collectibles. Income from the sale of collectibles may be taxed at a higher rate than other investments. Visit irs.gov or consult a certified public accountant for more information.
- Check out any coin dealers in a search engine online. Read about other people's experiences. Try to communicate offline if possible to clarify any details. In addition, contact your state Attorney General and local consumer protection agency. Checking with these organizations in the communities where promoters are located is a good idea, but realize that it isn't fool-proof: it just may be too soon for someone to realize they've been defrauded or to have lodged a complaint with the authorities.

TIP-OFFS TO RIP-OFFS

Scams in collectible coins generally involve false claims about grading, current value or buy back options.

False Grading Claims – Unscrupulous sellers of collectible coins often inflate the grade of their coins. Some dealers grade their coins in-house or through less-than-reputable grading services. Others create counterfeit grading documents or place lower grade coins in cases labeled with a higher grade. Walk away from the purchase if the case appears to have been opened, if documents appear to have been altered, or if a dealer won't show you the grading documents or let you examine the coin case before you buy.

False Claims about Current Value – Some dealers grade their coins accurately, but overprice them or mislead their customers about their value. For example, a dealer may charge $5,000 for an accurately graded $10 Indian gold piece, even though the current retail value of the coin may be $1,750.

False Claims about Buy Back Options – Many sellers of collectible coins offer "buy back" options to give buyers a sense of security in their investment. Dishonest sellers fail to honor the option, or fail to disclose commissions and other fees they attach to the option. In these cases, you may find that your true options are to hold the collectible coins or sell them at a loss on the open market.

INDEX